I0095380

Praise for *Bend, Don't Break*

"Through relatable stories, research-backed insights, and hands-on challenges, this book shows you how to evolve continuously without losing yourself, break free from resistance patterns that keep you stuck, and thrive alongside AI by embracing your uniquely human edge. This is a must-read for today's (and tomorrow's) leaders."

—Deborah Grayson Riegel, *Harvard Business Review* columnist, and bestselling author of *Go to Help* and *Overcoming Overthinking*

"In *Bend, Don't Break*, Matt West offers a timely, deeply human guide for navigating the transition we're all experiencing with AI and beyond. He reminds us that *adaptability isn't a skill— it's a system*—a way to stay grounded, grow through uncertainty, and lead ourselves and others with clarity and courage in a world of constant change."

—Charlie Hugh-Jones, leadership advisor, executive coach, and author of *Be More: What to Do When You Can't Do Any More!*

Bend, Don't Break

Bend, Don't Break

How to *Adapt* in the New World of Work

Matt A. West

GFB

Copyright © 2026 by Matt A. West

All rights reserved.

No part of this book may be reproduced, or stored in a
retrieval system, or transmitted in any form or by any means,
electronic, mechanical, photocopying, recording, or otherwise,
without express written permission of the publisher.

Without in any way limiting the author's and publisher's exclusive rights
under copyright, any use of this publication to "train" generative artificial
intelligence (AI) technologies to generate text is expressly prohibited.
The author reserves all rights to license uses of this work for generative
AI training and development of machine learning language models.

Some names and identifying details have been
changed to protect the privacy of individuals.

GFB

Published by GFB™, Seattle
www.girlfridayproductions.com

Produced by Girl Friday Productions

Cover design: Greg Mortimer
Production editorial: Kylee Hayes
Project management: Kristin Duran

Image credits: cover, Jian Fan/iStock (waves),
ALEKSANDR ARTIMOVICH/iStock (paper)

ISBN (paperback): 978-1-967510-26-9
ISBN (ebook): 978-1-967510-27-6

Library of Congress Control Number: 2025921404

First edition

For Gavin, Abe, Ella, and Jay:
Who you are is enough.
Who you're becoming is awesome.

Contents

Cultivate the Core Five

Grow in Beta

Introduction

"None of this really matters. We're all going to lose our jobs to AI anyway."

That comment, made by one of my coaching clients, stopped me in my tracks. It wasn't just the words that struck me. It was the resignation, the defeat, the feeling of being powerless against change.

It wasn't the first time I'd heard a version of that line. And it won't be the last. People are overwhelmed. Not just by AI but by the unrelenting pace of change: the meetings, the pivots, and the expectations to do more with less, faster than ever before.

And somewhere along the way, the things we used to rely on—hard work, experience, knowing the right answers—stopped feeling like enough.

This book is about what to do when that happens. It's about how to adapt when everything around you is changing faster than you can keep up. And it's about how to do it without burning out, selling out, or shutting down.

Why I Wrote This Book

Here's a secret I don't often admit: I've struggled with change myself.

I've spent my career coaching leaders, teams, and professionals through transformation, some who chose to change, others who had change thrust upon them. And despite devoting much of my time helping organizations and professionals build adaptability, I've resisted change at times, both personally and professionally. I confused persistence with inflexibility, a hard work ethic with rigidity. I clung to familiar approaches even when they stopped working.

For instance, I found myself using the same parenting strategies I'd relied on for years—routines, rewards, consequences—even when they clearly weren't working anymore. As my kids became teenagers, how I parented began to backfire. I was doubling down on rules, when what they actually needed was connection, empathy, and for me to grow alongside them. It took me a while to realize that my persistence, while well intentioned, had turned into rigidity.

Each time change forced me to adapt, I initially fought against it. That is, until I learned that adaptability isn't about abandoning what works. It's about knowing when and how to flex.

That lesson shaped the way I coach, lead, and live. It's also why I wrote this book.

I've seen firsthand how adaptability transforms careers and organizations. I've helped professionals navigate AI disruptions, industry shifts, and leadership changes by building the skills to use change to their advantage.

Knowing you need to change is one thing. Actually doing it is another. That's where this book comes in. I wrote it to bridge the gap between intention and action. The strategies and exercises included aren't just theoretical. They're real-world tools that have helped my clients, my colleagues, and me.

This isn't a book about AI. But AI is one of the unmistakable forces pushing all of us to rethink how we work, what we value, and where we go next. You'll see references to AI throughout this book. Not because it's the only thing changing the world of work, but because it's the biggest. More importantly, it's changing the *people* doing the work.

That means *adaptability* isn't just a buzzword. It's a requirement.

But what most people misunderstand about adaptability is that it's not a single skill. It's not something you either have or don't. It's a system. One that you can understand, build, and grow.

That system is what this book is all about.

And here's what I've learned, again and again: It's not the smartest or strongest people who thrive through change. It's the ones who are willing to stretch, to evolve, to reimagine how they work and who they are, without losing what grounds them. It's the ones who adapt.

What You'll Learn

We'll start by looking at why so many of us feel stuck. You'll discover how to identify the hidden patterns that hold you back and how to rewire them with small, intentional moves. You'll develop five core adaptability skills: curiosity, vulnerability, agility, flexibility, and resilience. And you'll see how to build those skills into daily habits so they serve you in real moments, not just in theory.

This isn't only about professional growth. It's about what happens when the pressure mounts and the old ways stop working. Without adaptability, stress builds, energy drains, and eventually something gives.

This book will show you how to navigate pressure without losing your footing. How to stay rooted when everything around you is in motion. How to respond, recover, and grow.

You'll learn how to meet change with clarity, not chaos, and how to stretch just enough without snapping under the weight of what's next.

In short, you'll learn how to bend without breaking.

How to Use This Book

Bend, Don't Break will help you find the sweet spot between persistence and flexibility. In the following pages, you'll learn practical strategies for becoming more adaptable on the job. This book is built for action. But it's also built to be flexible, much like the topic it covers. You can engage with it in a few different ways:

Read it cover to cover
Follow the complete journey from front to back. Each chapter builds on the last, moving through methods, strategies, and activities.

Skip to what you need
Each chapter stands alone as a closer look into one aspect of adaptability. Facing a career transition? Jump to Chapter 24. Struggling with complacency on the job? Chapter 11 has you covered.

Try your luck
Sometimes the insights we need most aren't the ones we'd consciously choose. Flip to a random chapter and try one of the challenges. You might surprise yourself.

Use it as a reference
Think of this book as a tool kit. Return to it whenever you need help with a specific situation. Each chapter can be revisited as you strengthen your adaptability muscles.

Practice the exercises
Adaptability isn't built by reading; it's built by doing. Try the challenges, track your progress, and stretch your comfort zone one step at a time.

Share and discuss
Adaptability grows through practice and conversation. Share what you learn with your colleagues, try the challenges with your team, and discuss what works for you.

Whether you're a seasoned executive, a mid-career professional, or someone just starting out, this book is for anyone who is navigating real, human moments of change. It's for people who are overwhelmed by complexity, unsure what's next, or just tired of pretending like they've got it all figured out. (Hint: None of us have it all figured out.)

Are You Ready?

You don't have to change *everything* about yourself to become more adaptable. In fact, real adaptability starts with knowing what *not* to change: your values, your purpose, your strengths. That's what keeps you grounded. That's what allows you to bend.

So if you're ready to build something new—not just in your job, but in how you respond to uncertainty itself—you're in the right place.

Because here's the truth: AI is here. It's changing your job, reshaping what's required, what's valued, and what's possible. And those who can adapt, flex, grow, and evolve? They're the ones who will shape the future of work.

Are you ready to bend without breaking? To flex without snapping? To stretch your skills, expand your mindset, and bounce back stronger than ever?

Good. Because the future isn't something that happens to you.

It's something you create.

And it starts right here, right now.

WHY WE BREAK

1

The End of Expertise

I like my routines. I like knowing what to expect. And I definitely don't like it when technology decides to "improve" itself without consulting me first. (Not cool, technology, not cool.)

A few years ago, my favorite music practice app, the one I used daily at the time without even thinking, completely overhauled its interface overnight. One afternoon, I sat down, ready to go through my usual piano practice session, and instinctively tapped where the start button had always been. Nothing happened. Confused, I tapped again. And again. My brain short-circuited for a second as I stared at the unfamiliar screen, my muscle memory now useless.

I spent an embarrassing amount of time searching for a single button that used to be right there, until I finally broke down and googled, "Where did the button go?"

It was a small, stupid thing, but it threw my entire routine into a tailspin. I'd gotten so comfortable with the old layout that I didn't think about what I was doing. I just acted. That habit saved me time and effort, which is exactly why we all do certain things on autopilot. We instinctively reach for the light switch in the dark, type our phone passcodes without looking, drive the same route to work without noticing the turns.

But this time, my brain's autopilot failed me. And I didn't like it. No one warned me it would change. No one asked me if I wanted a new layout. It just happened.

And the worst part? No amount of frustration made the app revert to its old design, just like no amount of resistance stops change in the workplace. Wishing things would stay the same won't stop them from evolving. It just makes you the last person to adapt.

Why Adaptability Is the New Competitive Edge

Not long ago, career success was built on expertise, experience, and execution. If you mastered your craft, built a solid reputation, and put in the hard work, you could count on a steady career trajectory.

That's no longer the reality.

The ground beneath us keeps shifting, and the pace of change is accelerating. Entire industries are being disrupted overnight. AI is transforming the way we work in ways most of us are still struggling to understand. Jobs that were once stable are evolving at breakneck speed. Skills that once guaranteed employment are becoming obsolete.

Recent research shows that while AI fluency is quickly becoming the most in-demand skill for professionals, it's not the only one. The demand for human strengths like adaptability, conflict navigation, and innovative thinking is also rising fast. The common thread? These are the capabilities machines can't easily replicate. The ones that make us not just useful, but uniquely valuable in an AI-driven world.

Adaptability has gone from a nice-to-have to a must-have. It's not just another bullet point on a résumé. It's the foundation that allows every other skill to evolve.

According to LinkedIn and Microsoft, adaptability is one of the most in-demand traits globally. And it's especially prized in a world where AI and automation continue to accelerate workplace transformation.

The takeaway? Expertise might get you in the door, but adaptability is what helps you stay in the room.

What's the Difference?

People often use the terms *flexibility*, *agility*, and *adaptability* interchangeably, but I believe they're not the same. And understanding the difference matters.

Flexibility is about being open. It's the willingness to pivot when plans change, to shift course, to accommodate new information. Flexible professionals are receptive, collaborative, and good at adjusting on the fly.

Agility is about speed. It's the ability to move quickly and decisively, especially when time is short and the pressure is high. Agile professionals move quickly and purposefully while others are still hesitating.

Adaptability is about growth. It's your capacity to absorb change, evolve your thinking, and apply new behaviors in response to a shifting environment. It's the deeper, slower, and more strategic muscle that allows you to grow through change, not just survive it.

Here's how I think about it:

- Flexibility helps you adjust.
- Agility helps you move.
- Adaptability helps you grow.

Agility and flexibility are useful. But without adaptability? You're just reacting. Sprinting in the wrong direction. Bending without purpose. In a world shaped by AI, adaptability is what allows you to evolve with intention. It's not just about keeping up or staying open to change. It's about staying relevant, grounded, and ready for whatever comes next. Adaptability is what keeps you growing when the ground shifts beneath your feet.

The Myth of Expertise

For years, we were told to become experts. To specialize. To get really, really good at one thing. And that made sense in a world where the pace of change was manageable.

But the old playbook doesn't work anymore.

Today, being an expert isn't enough. In fact, it can be a liability. I call this phenomenon **Frozen Expertise**: when what you once mastered starts weighing you down instead of lifting you up. When you define your value by what you know, you become vulnerable the moment that knowledge becomes outdated.

That doesn't mean expertise has no value. But in today's world, what matters more is your ability to keep learning, unlearning, and reapplying what you know in new contexts. Adaptability makes your expertise elastic, able to stretch, combine, and connect in creative ways that stay relevant even as the world changes.

I've built a name for myself as a leadership and communications expert. And don't get me wrong: I'm proud of that. I've helped professionals communicate better, coach more effectively, lead with heart, and navigate the gray areas of work with more clarity and confidence.

But I've also caught myself gripping my own identity too tightly.

There were times I resisted new technology because that just wasn't how I worked then.

When the COVID lockdown hit, I clung to my in-person facilitation methods, hoping the digital shift would pass. I rolled my eyes at virtual whiteboards and online Post-its, frustrated by how unnatural it all felt. For months, I resisted, until I realized my resistance was draining more energy than learning something new ever would. So I jumped in. I learned the tools, rewired my approach, and discovered something surprising: Adaptability had less to do with the platforms and more to do with my willingness to learn.

That's when it clicked. The thing I was holding on to— my expertise—wasn't helping me anymore. It was getting in the way.

Expertise had become a trap. The more I clung to what I knew, the harder it became to grow.

Eventually, I decided to stop chasing expertise and start building something more sustainable: adaptability.

From Knower to Learner

This chapter isn't here to convince you to abandon your expertise. It's here to challenge you to expand it.

If you want to stay relevant, you have to shift from a knower mindset to a learner mindset. That shift unlocks a career edge that comes from staying curious, evolving your skills, and applying new ways of thinking even when the rules change.

Here are three ways you can do just that:

Ask more questions than you answer
In meetings or conversations, challenge yourself to ask at least one thoughtful question before offering your opinion. Start with prompts like "What led you to that approach?" or "What

do you think we're missing?" Questions signal openness and invite better thinking from everyone involved.

Stay curious, even when you feel confident

When you find yourself thinking, *I already know this,* pause and ask, "What else could be true here?" Seek out different perspectives, newer tools, or emerging trends, even in areas where you feel like you're the expert. It keeps your edge sharp and your mind open.

Reframe change as an opportunity to grow, not a threat to what you know

Instead of resisting what's unfamiliar, look at change as data. What's shifting, and why? What can you adjust, upgrade, or let go of? Make a habit of reflecting after changes, big or small, by asking, "What did I learn from that, and what will I do differently next time?"

Whether you're managing people, pitching clients, writing code, or leading a team through transformation, your ability to stay curious and adaptable will matter more than the depth of your résumé.

Adaptability doesn't mean letting go of everything you know. It means being rooted in what matters most and being willing to stretch beyond your habits.

Welcome to the end of expertise.

Let's build what comes next.

Your "End of Expertise" Challenges

This week, practice trading certainty for curiosity. Try one or more of the following exercises:

Reclaim Your Edge
Make a list of your top three to five professional skills or knowledge areas. Then ask:

- Which still serve me well?
- Which might be outdated or over-relied on?
- Where could I become a learner again?

The Curiosity Day
For one full workday, try this experiment: Instead of offering answers, ask questions. Notice how it shifts conversations and how others respond.

The Job Description Flip
Take your current job title and rewrite it, not based on your tasks, but on how you want to grow. Think about the qualities you're developing or the impact you want to have. For example: "Marketing Manager" might become "Curiosity Catalyst." This playful reframing can help you imagine new possibilities and step into a more expansive version of your role.

2

The Adaptability Paradox

Remember when you were a kid, and someone would ask, "What do you want to be when you grow up?" The implication was clear: Pick a career and stick with it.

Yeah, forget that.

Today's kids might grow up asking a different question: "What do I want to create next?"

Because most of the jobs they'll end up doing haven't been invented yet.

And even for adults, the pace of change means we don't just switch roles. We evolve. Not once, but again and again. Entire industries are transforming overnight. Roles that felt stable five years ago are now being automated, outsourced, or reimagined. And brand-new careers are emerging in their place.

So why is it so hard to be adaptable? Because comfort is compelling. And breaking out of familiar rhythms takes intention, not just willpower.

The Paradox of Adaptability

If change is inevitable and adaptability is the key to staying relevant, why do so many people resist it? The paradox is this: In order to bend, you need something to hold on to.

I live in Colorado, and I love the outdoors. There's something about being out on a trail, the crunch of dirt beneath my boots, the scent of pine filling the crisp mountain air, that makes me feel grounded. I try to hike at least once a week. It's my way of pressing pause, stepping away from the constant noise of work and life, and just being present.

But if you've ever spent time in Colorado, you know the weather can turn on you in an instant. One moment, the sky is blue, and the sun is warm on your skin. The next, dark clouds roll in over the peaks, the wind shifts, and you feel the temperature drop like a trapdoor opening beneath your feet. More than once, I've set out on a beautiful, sunny day only to find myself sprinting back to my car as a sudden hailstorm pummels the trail. It doesn't matter how prepared you think you are, the mountains have a way of reminding you who's really in charge.

I think about that every time I see a Colorado pine standing tall in the middle of a storm. The wind howls down from the Rockies, whipping through its branches, bending them in all directions. Sleet pelts its needles in winter, the scorching sun bakes its bark in summer, and sudden temperature swings push it to its limits. One day, a deep freeze. The next, a warm spell. But it doesn't break. It doesn't collapse. Why? Because it has strong roots.

The Adaptability of Trees and People

Adaptability is like a tree. A strong tree doesn't resist the wind—it moves with it. It bends, adjusts, and finds ways to endure, not by fighting the elements but by working with them.

Its roots run deep, anchoring it in place. Your roots—your purpose, values, and unique strengths—keep you grounded when everything around you is shifting. No matter how much the environment changes, a tree that is well rooted remains standing.

But staying rooted isn't enough. Trees also grow branches, flexible, resilient, and always reaching outward. Your adaptability skills, habits, and mindset are those branches. They allow you to stretch, adjust, and evolve without losing what makes you strong.

I see it every day living in Colorado. Whether it's the massive Colorado blue spruce outside my front window or the Douglas firs lining the trails in Arapahoe National Forest, the trees that last aren't just strong. They're specialized.

- Ponderosas have thick, fire-resistant bark that shrugs off wildfires. Their deep roots anchor them against powerful mountain winds.
- Aspens don't stand alone. They're connected underground, relying on each other to survive.
- Piñon pines and junipers thrive in the driest, rockiest terrain, pulling moisture from deep beneath the surface.

Some of Colorado's wildest weather swings come in the spring and fall. One day, it's warm and dry. The next, temperatures drop thirty to forty degrees, bringing heavy snowfall or freezing rain. Snow, hail, sleet, rain, heat, floods—sometimes all in the same week. If you don't like the weather, just wait a few minutes.

But the trees here don't fight the elements. They respond to them. They sway instead of snap. They shed needles when energy is scarce. They find subtle, seasonal ways to adjust without losing their form. That's what keeps them rooted through the chaos: constant, quiet adaptation.

It's a truth that even Charles Darwin understood. As business professor Leon C. Megginson famously summarized Darwin's thinking: It's not the strongest or the smartest species that survive, but the ones most responsive to change.

That's true of trees. It's true of ecosystems. And it's true of us.

The most adaptable professionals and organizations aren't the ones who panic at every shift or throw out everything they know. They're the ones who stay rooted in their values and strengths while adjusting their approach.

Being adaptable doesn't mean discarding everything familiar. It means knowing what keeps you grounded while allowing yourself to grow. It means understanding the difference between rigidity and resilience. Between stubbornness and strength. Between fear of change and the ability to grow through it.

Stability and Flexibility: Finding the Balance

Think about your own career. If you look back at all the roles you've had, chances are you didn't throw away everything you'd learned each time you started something new. You built on what you had. You took existing skills and applied them in new contexts.

Take my own career, for example. I've been a fast-food employee, waiter, musician, composer, graphic designer, creative director, communications consultant, team leader, client account executive, learning and development administrator, adjunct professor, meeting facilitator, presentation skills trainer, and executive coach. Quite the career buffet, right? But I wasn't randomly hopping from one thing to another. Each job taught me something new. Each shift helped me refine my skills and broaden my expertise. And ultimately, every role prepared me for the most important skill of all: adaptability.

If I had clung rigidly to one career path, insisting that I had to stick with what I originally set out to do, I wouldn't be where I am today. But if I had tossed everything out with each new role, treating every shift as a total reset, I wouldn't have grown, either.

There's a difference between jumping from job to job, hoping something sticks, and approaching each change as a chance to collect something useful: a skill, a perspective, a lesson. The former can leave you feeling scattered. The latter creates momentum.

What matters isn't how many turns your path takes but how intentionally you walk it.

The key is balancing stability and flexibility. Knowing what to carry forward and what to leave behind. Understanding which parts of your experience ground you and which ones need to stretch.

When Strength Becomes a Weakness

Many of us confuse rigidity with positive traits like tenacity, determination, and persistence. After all, shouldn't we push through challenges? Shouldn't we stay committed to our goals?

Yes—but there's a big difference between healthy persistence and harmful rigidity. Grit is about staying committed to your goals while being open to different ways of reaching them. It means holding on to your values while being willing to reassess your opinions when new information comes to light. Rigidity, on the other hand, means clinging to an approach even when it's not working or no longer true.

Think of a running back on the football field. The play calls for him to hit the left sideline, but there's a defender in his path. Rigidity is trying to bulldoze straight through. Adaptability is cutting right, dodging the tackle, maybe even flipping the ball to a teammate. The goal stays the same, but the path changes.

Being adaptable doesn't mean chasing every trend or saying yes to every new approach. Instead, it means thoughtfully evaluating changes through the lens of your values and long-term growth.

Ask yourself:

- Does this change align with who I am and what's most important to me?
- Will adapting to this shift help me serve my long-term goals?

The most successful people I know combine strong commitment with flexible actions. They know when to persist and when to adapt. They understand that adaptability makes their determination more effective, not less.

The Strength of Rooted Adaptability

Individuals and organizations face the same challenge. The ones that thrive through change aren't the ones who react impulsively to every new development. They're the ones who understand their core strengths (their "roots") while having the agility to adapt (their "branches").

For individuals, your roots might be:

- Your purpose
- Your core values
- Your unique strengths

And your branches—the part that flexes and adapts— might be:

- How you apply your skills in different industries
- How you learn new technologies and tools
- How you shift your mindset to embrace change instead of fearing it

For organizations, your roots might be:

- Your mission and values
- Your company culture
- Your core competencies

And your organizational branches might be:

- How you evolve your business model
- How you integrate emerging technologies
- How you develop and empower your workforce

Adaptability isn't about being untethered or going wherever the wind blows. It's about having a strong foundation that allows you to grow in new directions without losing what makes you strong. We'll dive deeper into what to root to, and what not to root to, in Chapter 8.

But knowing what to hold on to isn't always easy, especially when what's shifting is your sense of self. That's what we'll explore next.

Your "Adaptability Paradox" Challenges

This week, explore what keeps you grounded and what might need to shift. Try one or more of the following exercises:

Name What Grounds You

Make a short list of what keeps you steady during change. These might include values, strengths, or trusted relationships. Then ask:

- Which of these roots truly support my growth?
- Are any of them actually keeping me stuck?

The Branch Inventory

List a few recent changes in your work or life. For each one, reflect:

- Did I bend or resist?
- How could I have approached the change with more flexibility or intention?

Your Adaptability Tree Map

Draw a quick diagram (or just visualize) your adaptability tree:

- Label the roots: core values, strengths, and non-negotiables.
- Label the branches: new skills, habits, or shifts you're working on. This helps you

visualize where you're strong and where
you might be brittle.

The Bend Detector
Choose one small thing this week that annoys you or
disrupts your rhythm—a delayed meeting, a tech hic-
cup, a last-minute change of plans. When it happens,
pause and ask:

+ What am I holding on to? A need for
  control? Certainty? A specific outcome or
  timeline?
+ What can I flex? My expectations? My approach? The story I'm telling myself about
  how this *should* go?

This builds real-time adaptability, one bend at a
time.

3

Identity Protection

We like to think we're resistant to change because change is hard. Because it's unfamiliar. Because it's uncomfortable.

But often, the real reason we resist change is because it threatens who we believe we are.

It's not just about the work. It's about **Identity Protection**.

When we're asked to do something new at work—learn a new platform, lead a different team, use AI to analyze data—the resistance we feel isn't just cognitive. It's emotional. It's not just *I don't want to do this.* It's also *This isn't me.*

The Pull of Self-Preservation

Take the mountain lion, one of the Rocky Mountains' most adaptive predators. In the wild, it's a master of stealth and survival, knowing how to stalk, when to hide, and how to navigate the region's rugged terrain.

Growing up in Utah, I was constantly warned to watch for mountain lions when I was riding my mountain bike or hiking. There were signs posted at trailheads, stories passed down from adults, and the ever-present reminder: "You probably won't see it until it's too late."

I remember one ride in particular, gliding downhill on a shaded bike trail in Bell Canyon, when I heard something rustle in the brush. My heart jumped into my throat. It was probably a rabbit, or maybe just the wind. But the fear was real. It wasn't just fear of being attacked. It was fear of being unprepared. Of being vulnerable to something I couldn't see or control.

That fear stuck with me. And in some ways, it still does.

What I didn't realize then but I see now is how similar that fear is to the fear many of us feel at work. Not of physical danger, but of something just as threatening: losing control, losing relevance, or losing the identity we've worked hard to protect. It's the same instinct to brace, to avoid, to resist, even when the threat is invisible.

What's remarkable is how mountain lions have adapted as humans have increasingly moved into their territory. Some have shifted their hunting patterns to become more nocturnal and avoid human activity. Others have changed their ranges entirely, seeking new paths through shrinking wilderness.

They didn't abandon who they are; they adjusted how they operate. They protected what mattered most—their ability to survive—by flexing their behavior.

And that's exactly what we're being asked to do in the workplace. We aren't facing predators in the brush. But we are navigating invisible threats to our identity: how we're seen, valued, and understood. Like the mountain lion, we protect what's core. But adaptability doesn't mean letting it go. It means learning to express it in new ways.

Across the natural world, survival and adaptation aren't

opposing forces. They work in tandem. From the smallest insects to the largest predators, every creature is wired to protect what matters most and to evolve when the conditions demand it. That's how ecosystems endure. Species don't just fight to survive. They adapt to thrive. Birds change migration patterns. Bears adjust hibernation rhythms. Even mountain lions evolve their habits as their habitats change.

That's the balance we're all trying to strike.

In the natural world, survival isn't about never changing. It's about changing in ways that preserve what matters most.

Humans aren't all that different. When we're faced with change, our brains are wired to protect our sense of self. It's not just about conserving energy or avoiding discomfort. It's about preserving identity. This is why change often feels so personal, even when it's just a new project or a software rollout.

We aren't resisting the task. We're resisting what the task might say about who we are.

Take Allison, for example. For years, she was known for creating a beautifully detailed custom report, one that required deep institutional knowledge, technical skill, and long hours every month. It wasn't just a task. It was her signature. So when a new dashboard tool automated most of what she did, Allison didn't just feel replaced; she felt erased. If she didn't own the report anymore, did she still matter? Did people still see her as someone uniquely valuable?

What Allison experienced is something many professionals face today: the slow onset of Frozen Expertise. When the value we worked so hard to build no longer fits the world we're working in, the fear runs deeper than skills. It touches identity.

That's the real fear beneath many workplace changes. Not just *Can I do this?* but *Am I still needed?* Like the mountain lion, we cling to what defines us. But true adaptability isn't about letting go of who we are. It's about learning how to protect our value by expressing it in new ways.

How Identity Shapes Our Reaction to Change

We all carry invisible identity statements that shape how we work:

- I'm the expert.
- I'm the one people count on.
- I'm the creative one.
- I'm not good with technology.
- I'm the hardest worker on my team.
- I'm a perfectionist.
- I don't do things halfway.

Those identities can be strengths. But they can also become cages.

I once coached a client who had spent their entire career in marketing. They were known for it. They had built a reputation, a network, even a sense of pride around that title.

But the organization was shifting. Their new role required them to lead broader communications strategy—internal, external, executive—and the word *marketing* was being removed from their job title.

On paper, it was a promotion. More visibility. More influence. More impact.

But emotionally? It felt like a demotion. Like they were losing part of themselves.

They weren't resisting the work. They were resisting the loss of identity.

We worked through it together, slowly untangling who they are from what their title says. What emerged was a more integrated sense of self. Not limited to a label, but grounded in values, skills, and a capacity to lead beyond the old boundaries.

This is the real work of adaptability.

When change arrives, we're asked to challenge those identity stories. That can feel threatening. Even dangerous.

It's easier to defend our current identity than it is to stretch into a new one.

But the truth is, the people who thrive in times of change aren't the ones with the most fixed sense of self. They're the ones who know how to evolve their identity without losing their values.

Why AI Hits Us So Personally

It's easy to think of artificial intelligence as just another tool. But for many professionals, AI represents something deeper: the fear that their hard-earned expertise, instincts, or creative talents are being devalued.

According to research from the World Economic Forum and multiple workplace studies, the top concerns employees cite around AI adoption aren't purely technical; they're emotional. Loss of value. Loss of uniqueness. Loss of identity.

Whether you're a copywriter, strategist, accountant, or coach, AI challenges more than your workflow. It challenges your identity.

If you've built your career on being the person who thinks fast, solves creatively, or sees the patterns others miss, what does it mean when a machine can do that too?

That's not just a practical challenge. It's an emotional one.

The risk is that you'll cling to who you used to be and miss the opportunity to become who you need to be now or who you're capable of becoming next.

In the next chapter, we'll explore why adaptability isn't just one thing but a system. One you can learn, build, and strengthen.

Your "Identity Protection" Challenges

This week, challenge your self-concept and expand your adaptability edge. Try one or more of the following exercises:

The "I Am" List
Write down three to five "I am . . ." statements that describe your identity at work. For example:

- I am the calm voice in a crisis.
- I am the creative spark in brainstorms.
- I am the fixer.
- I am the go-to expert.

The Evolution Reflection
Choose one of your identity statements and ask:

- When did I first start believing this?
- How has it served me?
- Where might it now be limiting me?

The Identity Expansion
Write a revised version of one of your identity statements that keeps your core but opens space to grow. For example:

From "I'm the expert" to "I'm always learning and sharing what I know."

4

How to Not Break

Not long ago, a client of mine said something that stuck with me.

"It's not that I don't want to change. It's just that I'm already at my breaking point."

She wasn't being dramatic. She was being honest. She was smart, committed, deeply empathetic, and completely exhausted. Her team was going through a restructure. Her job responsibilities had tripled. And just as she started to find her footing again, her organization rolled out a suite of new AI tools with an urgent directive: Adapt now or get left behind.

She wasn't resisting change because she didn't understand it. She was resisting because she was already overloaded.

And that's the part of adaptability we don't talk about enough.

The Hidden Cost of Constant Change

We often celebrate adaptability like it's a badge of honor. Be flexible. Stay agile. Embrace the pivot. But the reality is, when you're living through wave after wave of change—especially the kind you didn't ask for—adaptability can feel like a burden instead of a gift. At some point, you stop feeling like a brave sailor and start feeling seasick.

Even when change is technically "good"—a promotion, a new tool that saves time, a more efficient process—it still costs energy. Cognitive energy. Emotional energy. Time. Focus. Trust.

And when those costs keep stacking up, something eventually gives. It might be a loss of motivation. Or energy. Or health. Or confidence. Or simply your ability to care as much as you used to.

Adaptability without care doesn't just cause burnout. It causes erosion. A slow wearing down of the parts of you that once felt strong.

When AI Is the Tipping Point

For many people, the arrival of AI in the workplace has triggered a full-blown identity crisis.

Suddenly, the work you've mastered feels like it's being handed off to a machine. The skills you built over decades feel like they're depreciating faster than you can keep up. The things that used to define your value—speed, accuracy, insight—are now being done in seconds by something that doesn't blink, sleep, or second-guess itself.

Even if your job is safe, it may no longer feel the same. And even if you're trying to learn, the pace of change can leave you feeling like you're constantly behind.

It's no wonder so many professionals report feeling anxious, unmotivated, or emotionally disconnected. The risk isn't just technological obsolescence. It's psychological burnout.

And all this is happening at a time when our systems, both human and organizational, are already stretched to the limit.

According to Microsoft, 80 percent of professionals say they don't have the time or energy to do their jobs, and nearly half describe their work as chaotic or fragmented. People are juggling nonstop pings, unexpected messages, and unpredictable schedules, averaging 275 interruptions a day—that's one every two minutes during work hours!

In other words, the speed of business is outpacing the capacity of people.

AI has the potential to ease that burden. But unless it's paired with a rethinking of how we work—not just faster but smarter—it risks becoming one more pressure point instead of a path to relief.

That's why adaptability matters more than ever.

What Breaking Looks Like

Breaking doesn't always mean collapse. Sometimes it shows up as overcommitment. Or procrastination. Or emotional detachment. Or endless busyness that numbs instead of moves you forward.

You may recognize some of these signs in yourself:

- You feel reactive, like you're just trying to get through the day.
- You dread opening your inbox, not because of the contents but because of the pressure it represents.
- You're so consumed with getting things done that you've stopped thinking about whether they still matter.

- You feel guilty for not being more excited about "innovation."

Sometimes, the most adaptable thing you can do is admit you're overwhelmed.

You Can't Bend Without Support

Trees don't stand alone. Even the strongest ones have root systems that intertwine underground, stabilizing each other in ways we can't see. Aspens thrive because they're connected. Pines withstand storms because their roots are deep and wide.
You don't need to handle everything by yourself.
Support systems aren't a sign of weakness. They're the reason people, and trees, don't snap under pressure.
That support might look like:

- A trusted colleague who gets what you're going through
- A manager who makes space for honest conversations, not just efficient ones
- A partner or friend who reminds you that you're more than your output
- A moment of stillness you claim for yourself before the next wave hits

Adaptability isn't always about being fast or fearless.
When the storm hits the hardest, it's about being open to help.

How to Stay Adaptable Without Burning Out

Before we dive into the four strategies of the **Adaptability System**, we need to address something essential: You don't need to tough it out to be adaptable. You need to build systems that keep you steady while you stretch.

Here are a few truths I come back to when I feel myself fraying:

Burnout isn't a personal failure. It's a systemic signal.

We tend to internalize exhaustion like it's a flaw in our character. I tend to do this myself. *If I was stronger, more organized, more focused, I wouldn't be this tired.* But burnout is rarely just about capacity. It's about mismatch: too many demands, not enough support. Too many shifts, not enough space to recover. When you're constantly adjusting to external change without time to process, the whole system tends to break down. That doesn't mean you're broken. It means your environment is asking too much, too fast, and with too little margin for error.

Your exhaustion is a message. Listen to it.

Rest is not a luxury. It's a prerequisite for insight.

We glorify hustle and idolize endurance. But insight doesn't come from urgency. It comes from stillness. When your nervous system is on high alert, your brain can't access the same creative, strategic, reflective thinking you need to solve complex problems. Insight lives in the quiet moments: the walk between meetings, that morning shower epiphany, the deep breath before responding.

Rest isn't what you do after the work is done. It's what makes the work possible. Rest is strategic. Say it with me: "Rest is strategic."

Resistance is not always bad. It's often a clue.

When you feel resistance to something, don't be too quick to discount or override it. Ask what your resistance is trying to protect. Sometimes resistance is fear dressed up as control. Sometimes it's your intuition alerting you to a misalignment— between your values and your environment, your energy and your obligations. Instead of shaming yourself for dragging your feet, get curious. What's underneath the hesitation? What are you afraid of losing? What are you needing to grieve?

In Chapter 10, we'll unpack these kinds of resistance loops in more detail. But for now, just know: Resistance isn't the enemy. It's often a signal that something important might need tending.

Doing less can help you grow more.

Adaptability isn't about doing more, faster. It's about doing the right things with clarity and intention. When we try to adapt to everything all at once, we dilute our energy and delay our growth. The most adaptable people aren't juggling chaos; they're pruning with purpose. They pause. They edit. They get clear on what matters most and let the rest fall away.

Sometimes the next big leap doesn't come from pushing harder. It comes from creating space to choose wisely.

So how do we not break?

We stop pretending we're supposed to carry it all alone. We start noticing the signals before they become symptoms.

Because adaptability isn't about bracing harder; it's about bending smarter. And sometimes, the bravest move is to pause, reset, and ask for help.

Before we dive into the system that will help you adapt with more clarity and confidence, remember this:

You don't need to be superhuman to be adaptable.

You just need to be supported.

Your "How to Not Break" Challenges

This week, focus on strengthening your foundation. Try one or more of the following:

Rate and Reset
Rate your energy, focus, and emotional bandwidth on a scale of 1–10. Then ask:

- What's draining me most right now?
- What's one thing I can pause or hand off?

The Support Scan
Identify one person who helps you feel more grounded at work. Send them a quick note of appreciation or ask for a quick chat. You're not meant to bend alone.

The Small Stillness
Set a five-minute timer. No email. No phone. Just breathe. Notice what comes up: thoughts, feelings, tensions, distractions. That's data your system may be too busy to access otherwise. What are your brain and body trying to tell you?

HOW TO BEND

5

Adaptability Is Not a Skill

One of the biggest myths about adaptability is that it's a single skill you either have or you don't. That's like saying fitness is a single muscle. Or that creativity is one trick you learn and master forever.

Adaptability isn't a skill. It's a system.

And like any system, it has moving parts. When one part weakens or gets overlooked, the whole system gets sluggish. But when you strengthen each part—when you treat adaptability like a living, breathing organism—you unlock a career advantage that's resilient, responsive, and real.

The Problem with Skill Talk

The workplace loves to talk about skills: soft skills, hard skills, transferable skills, power skills, AI-proof skills. Heck, I can't count how many times I've led training workshops on communication, emotional intelligence, leadership presence, time management, all the "soft" stuff we often call leadership skills. And don't get me wrong: I believe deeply in their value. I've seen firsthand how those skills can transform a person's confidence, their relationships, their impact.

But over time, I started to notice something. You can teach someone how to speak up in a meeting, how to coach with empathy, how to delegate effectively. But if they're paralyzed by change, none of it sticks. The real barrier isn't usually knowledge. It's what happens when the context shifts, the pressure mounts, or the rules change. That's when the old skills stop working—or get abandoned entirely.

That's why adaptability doesn't sit neatly in any of those boxes. Why? Because it's what allows all the other skills to grow, flex, or be reimagined.

It's not one thing; it's *everything*.

In my coaching work, I've seen high-performing leaders and ambitious professionals struggle not because they lacked technical knowledge, but because their approach to change was inconsistent. They could handle a leadership restructure but not a shift in tools. They could learn new tech but froze when their job title changed. They could handle market shifts but not the uncertainty of a new manager.

What made the difference? It was the ability to recognize what part of their adaptability system needed attention and then to strengthen it.

The System in Action

I once worked with a client who was known across her organization for her speed and decisiveness. She thrived in fast-paced environments, juggled competing priorities with ease, and had a reputation for getting things done when others froze. On paper, she looked like a textbook case of adaptability.

But when her company rolled out a long-term initiative focused on strategic transformation, she struggled. The pace was slower. The path was less defined. It required patience, ambiguity, and a willingness to lead without clear answers.

That's when the cracks started to show.

She wasn't short on agility. In fact, she could pivot and react with lightning speed. But she hadn't cultivated some of the other adaptability muscles: curiosity, vulnerability, and resilience. She avoided asking questions that might expose what she didn't know. She had trouble engaging in conversations that didn't have a clear outcome. And when things got messy, her instinct was to power through rather than pause and reflect.

In short, she had overdeveloped some parts of her system and completely overlooked others.

When we worked together, we started to map out what her adaptability system looked like. She was strong in action, weak in introspection. Quick to act, slow to reflect. Skilled at moving, uncomfortable with uncertainty.

The turning point came when she started seeing adaptability not as something she either had or didn't but as something she could build.

She started asking more questions. She began taking meaningful pauses before jumping into action. And she began to treat every ambiguous moment as an opportunity to grow.

It didn't change her personality, but it completely changed her approach.

The Adaptability System

In this book, you'll learn to build your adaptability system through four interlocking strategies:

- Root to the Right Things
- Prune the Loops
- Cultivate the Core Five
- Grow in Beta

Each one targets a different layer of your adaptive capacity. We'll explore each one in detail in the next section of the book. For now, think of these as the building blocks of your adaptability system: a structure you can grow, prune, and strengthen as your environment evolves.

Adaptability Can Be Strengthened

Adaptability isn't a single skill you check off a list. It's a system you build over time. A combination of habits, mindsets, and choices that work together to help you navigate change. And like any system, it can be refined. Strengthened.

You develop it through small shifts, repeated often. You build it by experimenting, reflecting, adjusting, and repeating.

And the more often you run the system, the more naturally it runs on its own.

The most adaptable people I know aren't fearless. They're system-aware. They've learned how to:

- Notice what's throwing them off.
- Name the root cause of resistance.
- Apply tools instead of panic.
- Recenter on what matters.
- Make decisions with more clarity and less drama.

That's what this book will help you do.

Because in the new world of work, adaptability isn't just a buzzword. It's your foundation.

Your "Adaptability Is Not a Skill" Challenges

This week, take stock of the system behind your ability to adapt. Try one or more of the following challenges:

The Resistance Radar
Write down three recent situations where you felt friction, frustration, or fatigue at work. Ask:

+ What was I resisting?
+ What part of my adaptability system might have needed support?

The System Scan
Jot down quick notes on how strong you feel in each of these areas:

+ Anchored in values and purpose
+ Aware of patterns that keep you stuck
+ Practicing core adaptability skills such as curiosity, resilience, and vulnerability
+ Experimenting with change
+ Applying what you learn in everyday situations

Which area is your strongest? Which could use some love?

The Adaptability Timeline
Draw a timeline of your career and highlight the three biggest moments of change. What helped you adapt? What got in your way?

The System Post-it

Write this phrase somewhere visible: *My adaptability is a system, not a switch.* Why? Adaptability isn't something you just turn on but a practice you build, little by little. Notice what changes in your approach this week when you treat yourself like a whole system in motion.

6

The Adaptability System

I didn't set out to build a framework for adaptability. I stumbled into it by listening.

Workshop after workshop, coaching conversation after coaching conversation, I kept hearing the same themes from people trying to navigate change:

We want to adapt. But we're stuck. Tired. Spinning our wheels. Overwhelmed by the speed of everything and unsure what to do next.

One moment stands out.

I was working with a leadership team at a healthcare company, a group tasked with driving innovation. The irony? They were stuck. Their workflows were outdated. Their culture, rigid. And the person resisting change the most was the one who'd brought me in.

Every time someone suggested a new approach, the leader shut it down. The team looked around the room, quietly signaling what none of them wanted to say out loud: *We're not going anywhere until he lets go.*

Finally, one team member spoke up. She shared that, in her previous role, curiosity had been encouraged, even expected. But here? It felt risky. That cracked something open. Suddenly, everyone saw it: Their ways of working weren't just inefficient. They were actively blocking adaptability.

By the end of the session, the very leader who'd been pushing for change said something I'll never forget:

"So . . . the problem isn't out there? It's us?"

That moment was one of many that shaped what you're about to read. Not because it was dramatic, but because it was familiar. It reflected a pattern I'd seen across industries:

The biggest challenge isn't change. It's how we *respond* to it.

Some people shut down. Others scramble. A few adapt.

What separates them isn't title, talent, or tenure. It's the strength of their adaptability system.

What Is the Adaptability System?

The Adaptability System isn't a set of tips. It's not a list of hacks or habits.

It's a deeper structure made up of four strategies that, together, help you build real, lasting adaptability.

- **Root to the Right Things**—Build stability through your values and purpose.
- **Prune the Loops**—Identify the habits, assumptions, and patterns that keep you stuck.
- **Cultivate the Core Five**—Strengthen the five essential skills of adaptability: curiosity, vulnerability, agility, flexibility, and resilience.

- **Grow in Beta**—Rewire your default behaviors, shift your mindset, and apply what you're learning through fast, low-risk experiments in real time.

Each section that follows will unpack one of these strategies. They're designed to stand alone, but they work best together.

A Living Framework

Throughout the rest of this book, you'll see a simple but powerful visual: a tree.

Not just as a metaphor, but as a model. A system. A structure you can come back to again and again.

The tree is a living illustration of how the four strategies of the Adaptability System work together. Like any healthy tree, your adaptability needs both deep roots and strong, flexible branches.

- The **roots** represent your foundation: your purpose, values, and strengths.
- The **branches** represent how you stretch, grow, and respond to the world around you.

Here's how each part of the system maps to the tree:

- **Root to the Right Things** → The Roots
- **Prune the Loops**
- **Cultivate the Core Five** } The Branches
- **Grow in Beta**

The tree that represents the Adaptability System is a reminder that real adaptability is rooted. It's structured. And it's designed to grow with you.

Just like a tree adapts to wind, drought, or sudden frost, you'll learn to stretch without snapping, to grow without losing stability, and to respond to change without abandoning who you are.

So as you read, return to the tree. Use it to orient yourself. Notice which parts of your own system feel strong, and which ones could use more stretch, more grounding, or more attention.

Don't Just React—Build

A lot of people treat adaptability like a reaction: something they scramble for when the ground shifts. But real adaptability is built before you need it.

Remember the flip phone? It was simple, dependable, and it got the job done. Back in the day, I loved my Motorola StarTAC. I could call and text (as long as I didn't mind pressing the same button three times for a single letter).

And for a while, that was enough. Until it wasn't.

One day, my flip phone went from being an everyday essential to feeling like a relic. It wasn't broken. It still worked just as well as it always had. But the world had moved on.

In came the smartphone. And suddenly, what I once thought was cutting-edge felt about as useful as a brick.

The smartphone wasn't just a newer model; it was designed to evolve as technology advanced. It could update, install new apps, and adapt to my needs the moment they changed. It wasn't designed for the past. It was designed for *what might come next.*

That's the goal of the Adaptability System: not just to help you survive change but to stay relevant, useful, and confident in a world that never stops moving.

A Practice, Not a Program

As you explore each chapter, you'll find:

- Real-world stories of people applying adaptability in messy, modern workplaces
- Challenges you can try immediately
- Tools and prompts to help you move from insight to action

This isn't a linear journey. You don't need to master one element before starting the next. Some chapters will feel familiar. Others may challenge your default settings. All of them are designed to help you stretch with intention.

So before you dive in, take a moment. Ask yourself:

- Where in your life or work are you being asked to bend?
- What feels stuck, brittle, or outdated?
- What small shift might help you build your capacity to adapt?

Keep that in mind as you read.

And let's build a system that flexes, learns, and grows.

Your "Adaptability System" Challenges

This week, focus less on building out the details and more on noticing the system itself. Try one or more of the following:

Sketch Out Your Tree
Draw a rough version of your adaptability tree, with roots for your values and branches for how you flex. Leave space to expand as you move through the later chapters.

Spot the System
Think of a recent change. Which part of your system did you rely on the most—grounding values, pruning habits, building skills, or experimenting? Which part felt absent?

Set Your Goal
Complete this sentence: "I want to build my adaptability system so that I can _____." Keep this goal statement visible as a guide for the chapters ahead.

7

Assess Your Own Adaptability

Before we dive into building an adaptable system, let's take a moment to check in with the one you're already running.

Adaptability isn't just something you learn. It's something you *live*. But most of us haven't taken the time to pause and ask: *Where am I strong? Where am I stuck? Where am I stretching just enough to grow, and where might I be about to snap?*

That's what this chapter is for.

This isn't a personality quiz or a productivity score. It's a snapshot of your current capacity to adapt. You don't need to impress anyone. Just be honest with yourself. The more real you are, the more useful this will be.

The Adaptability System Self-Assessment

Instructions:

- Rate yourself on a scale of 1–5 for each statement:

  1 = Strongly Disagree
  5 = Strongly Agree

- Be honest. No one's watching.
- Total your score in each section to see which parts of your system are strongest and which ones could use a little reinforcement.

Root to the Right Things

How grounded are you in your purpose and values?

1. I have a clear sense of purpose that guides my work.
2. I use my core values to stay grounded when things get chaotic.
3. I can adapt without losing who I am.
4. I regularly reflect on whether my work aligns with what matters to me.
5. In stressful moments, I return to my deeper "why."

Score: ____ / 25

Prune the Loops

How aware are you of your patterns of resistance and avoidance?

1. I can spot when I'm stuck in unhelpful habits or mindsets.
2. I notice when I avoid discomfort—and I get curious about why.
3. I reflect on my reactions to change instead of just pushing through.
4. I recognize when I confuse busyness with progress.
5. I can name at least one behavior or mindset that limits my adaptability.

Score: _____ / 25

Cultivate the Core Five

How strong are your core adaptability skills: curiosity, vulnerability, agility, flexibility, and resilience?

1. I stay curious, especially when I feel certain.
2. I'm willing to admit what I don't know and ask for help.
3. I can move quickly and adjust when things shift unexpectedly.
4. I flex my approach based on different people or situations.
5. I bounce back from setbacks without losing momentum.

Score: _____ / 25

Grow in Beta

How well do you experiment, iterate, and learn in real time?

1. I try small changes instead of waiting for perfect plans.
2. I treat feedback as fuel—not as judgment.
3. I experiment with new tools, workflows, or ideas regularly.
4. I apply what I learn quickly, even if the outcome isn't guaranteed.
5. I see myself as a work in progress—not a finished product.

Score: ____ / 25

Total Score: ____ / 100

How to Read Your Results

This isn't about passing or failing; it's about noticing patterns.

- **85–100:** You've built a strong adaptability system. Keep stretching and notice where you're still rigid.
- **65–84:** You're in motion. Some areas are strong; others could use attention. Reinforce the weak spots.
- **45–64:** You're building the foundation. Focus on the sections where you feel the most resistance.
- **Below 45:** You're at the beginning. That's a powerful place to start. Growth happens here.

Reflect and Reset

Take a look at your individual section scores. Which element of the system feels like your greatest strength? Which feels like the one that's been quietly holding you back?

Don't stop at the category level. Dig into the individual statements. You might score high overall in a section like Cultivate the Core Five but still struggle with one core trait, like vulnerability or agility. Or maybe your lowest section overall is Grow in Beta, but the real friction isn't experimentation—it's feedback.

The truth is, your adaptability isn't one number. It's a pattern.

Maybe you're great at bouncing back from setbacks (resilience) but hesitate to ask for help (vulnerability). Maybe you love learning new tools (curiosity) but freeze when plans shift (flexibility). That matters. Those patterns show you *where to focus*, not just what to fix.

Use this self-awareness as a map for the chapters ahead. Each one is designed to strengthen a different part of your system. The goal is to help you expand where you're limited, reinforce where you're strong, and personalize your growth.

You don't need to be perfectly balanced. You just need to know what you're working with and what you want to build next.

Your "Assess Your Own Adaptability" Challenges

Whether you're anchored, drifting, brittle, or just beginning, here's how to put your results to work:

Spot the Strongest Branch
Which section scored highest? That's your adaptability advantage. Leverage it more intentionally.

Find the Brittle Spot
Which section scored lowest? That's your growth opportunity. Start small. Even a one-point improvement is movement.

Pick One Habit to Try This Week
Maybe it's asking more questions (curiosity), reflecting on what you might be resisting (Prune the Loops), or running a micro-experiment at work (Break Up with Perfect).

Track the Pattern
What triggers your rigidity? What conditions help you flex? Start noticing. Awareness is how systems evolve.

Revisit and Reassess
Bookmark this chapter. Retake the assessment in three months. Put it on your calendar. Watch how your adaptability tree grows.

ROOT TO THE
RIGHT THINGS

8

Choose Your Roots

I grew up with a crabapple tree in my backyard: small, scraggly, and honestly, a bit underwhelming compared to the towering junipers that lined our neighborhood. But it was *ours*. I used to climb it, lean against it, and sit in its crooked limbs when I wanted to daydream.

That little tree wasn't impressive, but it was stubborn. Year after year, no matter how harsh the Utah winters were or how many branches snapped under the weight of snow, it kept coming back. Spring after spring, new buds would appear. Some seasons, the fruit was plentiful. Others, not so much.

Not that it really mattered; the crabapples were *terrible*. Tart, bitter, and practically inedible.

But still, the tree produced them like it was doing us a favor.

Only years later did I realize what made it so resilient: its roots. Deep, tenacious roots that anchored it through the stormiest seasons, even when everything above the surface looked fragile.

Adaptability is a lot like that. We often focus on what's visible: skills, habits, results. But what allows us to bend without breaking is what lies beneath: our values, our purpose, our strengths.

Before you try to stretch, shift, or grow, you need to know what you're rooted in.

Rooted Adaptability

This is the first element of the Adaptability System, or the roots to the tree: **Root to the Right Things**. Because the ability to adapt isn't just about motion. It's about knowing what not to move.

Root to the Right Things

In a world where roles are shifting, tools are multiplying, and change is relentless, adaptability starts by choosing what grounds you and what doesn't.

You're Always Rooted to Something

Most people think of roots as something intentional: the values or purpose you choose to stand on.

But you're already rooted to something. Even if you haven't named it. Even if it's not serving you.

Sometimes we're rooted to things we never chose. Like a title we've outgrown, a process we're overly attached to, or an outdated belief about what makes us valuable. These roots form quietly—through repetition, routine, or fear—and often go unnoticed until they're tested.

For the past twenty years, I've kept two framed lists on my desk, one labeled "My Purpose," the other "My Values." I created them after reading *The 7 Habits of Highly Effective People* by Stephen Covey, a book that challenged me to get clear on what mattered most and to let those principles guide how I showed up at work and in life.

Having those lists close to where I make most of my important decisions has grounded me through more changes than I can count. They've helped me say yes when the right opportunities came along. And just as importantly, they've helped me say no when something wasn't aligned.

But they haven't stayed static.

Not long ago, my family and I made a significant life decision that shifted how we saw the world and our place in it. It challenged us to reexamine what we believe, what we stand for, and how we want to live. It wasn't a small adjustment. It asked us to look honestly at the difference between what we said we valued and how we were actually living.

So I reworked my purpose and values lists. Not dramatically, but deliberately. I made sure they reflected the version of me I was growing into, not just the one I'd been.

That's the thing about roots: You have to choose them. And when life shifts, you may need to choose again.

When the Ground Shifts Under Your Role

I once worked alongside a strategist who had built his career on in-person field research. He was known for drawing deep insights from conversations, translating stories into strategy, nuance into narrative.

Then the company rolled out a suite of digital tools: online panels, instant dashboards, data-scraping platforms. The kind of work that used to take him weeks could now be done in a few hours and, often, without him.

He didn't protest. He didn't complain. But he kept doing things the old way, slower, more manually. He still delivered good work, but it was clear he was falling behind.

He wasn't resisting change. He was protecting something deeper: his identity. He was caught in Frozen Expertise. He had unknowingly rooted himself not to purpose, but to process. And when that process became optional, his sense of worth started to unravel.

That's the cost of rooting to something without realizing it: It makes you fragile in a storm you never saw coming.

To stay relevant, he would have to re-root, not just react. And in the end, that's what he did. He chose to leave the company and take a new role elsewhere, one that still honored his strength for storytelling, but in a context that felt more aligned with how he worked best. It wasn't failure. It was a re-rooting.

Strong Roots Make You More Responsive

But here's the flip side, and this is where rooting becomes powerful: The most adaptable people I know aren't constantly chasing the next trend. They're grounded.

They have a strong internal compass. They know what they stand for, so when the landscape changes, they're not spinning. They're responding. Quickly, clearly, and without losing themselves.

When the stakes are high or the pressure is on, the people who move with clarity are the ones with the deepest roots.

Roots don't make you slow. They make you sure.

What You Root to Matters

So what are you rooted to?

When everything around you is changing, what you're rooted to becomes the difference between evolving and unraveling.

If your roots are weak—or if you've unintentionally anchored yourself to the wrong things—you'll find yourself resisting change, clinging to control, or swimming against the tide.

To build rooted adaptability, start by being deliberate about what holds you steady and what doesn't deserve that power anymore.

This isn't just about individuals. It applies to teams, departments, and entire organizations. Everyone, and every system, is rooted to something. The question is whether it's helping you grow or keeping you stuck.

For Individuals: Root to These

Your Purpose

Your purpose is the deeper "why" behind your work. It provides clarity when things feel chaotic and continuity when roles or tools change. Purpose is the thread that helps you evolve without losing direction. Maybe your purpose is to create clarity in complexity. Or to help others feel heard. Or to solve problems that matter.

Your Core Values

Your values are the principles that shape how you work, lead, and respond under pressure. They don't shift with technology or trends. They are your foundation, and they become even more essential during change. You might value honesty, courage, kindness, excellence, or inclusion. Whatever they are, your values help guide your choices when the path forward isn't clear.

Your Unique Strengths

Your unique strengths represent your human edge in the workplace. They are not just tasks you can perform but qualities like empathy, judgment, creativity, and curiosity that set you apart. These strengths move with you throughout your career, even as specific roles and tools continue to shift and evolve.

For Individuals: Don't Root to These

Your Title or Status

Titles can change, sometimes overnight. If your identity is built on a job title or position, you become vulnerable the moment that label is no longer relevant.

Tools, Platforms, or Routines
Familiar systems may feel comforting, but they are not the same as values. If you root your worth to a particular tool or process, you'll struggle to grow when it's time to change or upgrade.

The Past Version of Yourself
Growth means evolving, even outgrowing your old self. Clinging to who you were can hold you back from becoming who you're meant to be next.

For Organizations: Root to These

Your Mission and Values
A clear mission and a shared set of values are what provide coherence and direction through complexity. These should remain steady even as business models, structures, or technologies evolve.

Your Culture
Culture includes your shared behaviors, mindsets, and ways of working. A strong culture supports adaptability by empowering learning, trust, and collaboration, not just efficiency.

Your Core Competencies
These are the fundamental strengths that make your organization unique. They should guide decisions about what to protect, what to evolve, and where to grow.

For Organizations: Don't Root to These

Business Models That No Longer Fit
Legacy revenue streams or outdated offerings may feel familiar, but clinging to them out of loyalty or ease can block innovation and long-term relevance.

Tools That Once Worked Well
Even high-performing systems expire. Rooting to a specific tool or process too tightly can prevent your teams from finding better, more adaptive solutions.

Org Structures That Prioritize Control over Growth
Rigid hierarchies and slow decision-making can stifle innovation. Organizations rooted to status, power, or control tend to resist change and often break under pressure.

Adaptability is about building a strong foundation that allows you to stretch, respond, and grow, all without losing what makes you strong.

When your roots are right, everything else can evolve around you.

Your "Choose Your Roots" Challenges

Try one or more of the following to identify what's anchoring you and to build stronger, more flexible roots.

The Values Conversation
Choose one colleague or friend whose career you admire. Ask them: "What values have anchored you when everything else changed?" Write down one insight you want to apply to your own career.

The Purpose Filter
Before your next big decision, ask:

- Does this align with what matters most to me?
- Am I doing this because it's right or because it's familiar?

The Re-Rooting Exercise
Think of a recent moment when you felt irrelevant, sidelined, or resistant.
Ask:

- What part of my identity felt threatened?
- What deeper value or strength was I trying to protect?
- How might I express that same strength in a different, more flexible way?

The Three-Root Statement
Finish this sentence:

I root myself to _____, _____, and _____.

Save it. Revisit it. Use it when everything around you feels like it's moving too fast.

9

Build Your Inner Capacity

If you want to adapt on the outside, you need strength on the inside.

It's not enough to root to your purpose or values. You also need to build the internal capacity to stay calm, curious, and clear when things start to shake.

Because when pressure hits, your adaptability will come from how well you manage what you feel, what you fear, and what you choose to do next.

I've seen this moment play out with professionals at every level, from first-year associates to senior leaders.

Everything seems fine . . . until something unexpected happens. A project falls apart. A team member snaps. A client ghosts. A budget is cut. A tool breaks. A plan unravels.

And suddenly, the person who was calm and composed is flooded with frustration, anxiety, or paralysis.

What shows up in those moments isn't about skill; it's

about capacity. Your adaptability in a crisis depends on the emotional, cognitive, and psychological resources you've built when things were calm.

What Is Inner Capacity?

Inner capacity is your ability to stay grounded when everything around you is pushing you off balance. It's made up of quiet, internal strengths that don't show up on performance reviews but shape everything about how you lead, communicate, and adapt under pressure. And while it can look like confidence on the outside, it's often something else entirely:

- The ability to notice your emotional state before it hijacks you
- The presence of mind to stay focused instead of overwhelmed
- The self-control to sit with discomfort instead of rushing to react

You don't build this overnight. But you can build it.

And the people who do are the ones who respond to uncertainty with perspective, not panic.

That said, not everyone accesses that sense of groundedness in the same way.

For some people, especially those navigating chronic stress, mental health challenges, or trauma, nervous system regulation isn't as simple as a few deep breaths or a mindset shift. Some have learned to function while dysregulated, operating in a low-grade state of freeze, fight, or hypervigilance. If that's your experience, know this: Everything in this chapter still applies. But it may take more time, more support, or more care to fully build these capacities. That doesn't make you less adaptable. It just makes your system more layered and more worthy of compassion.

Practice Makes . . .

You've probably heard the phrase "Practice makes perfect"— it's a favorite of music teachers everywhere.

I've always hated that phrase.

Perfect isn't the goal. And it's not realistic, something we'll explore in Chapter 22.

Instead, I try to remind myself, *Practice makes permanent*.

By working on something every day, it becomes part of who you are, not just something you do when it's convenient.

I try to work on my own inner capacity every day. Some days, I'm grounded and present, able to take a breath before reacting, stay focused in a tough moment, or respond to pressure with clarity. Other days? I lose my footing. I get flustered, distracted, or stuck in my head.

But the point isn't perfection; it's practice. Practice that makes permanence, turning effort into habits and habits into who you are.

The more I commit to building inner space, the more I notice when I'm about to drift or snap. And even if I miss the moment, I know how to come back faster than I used to.

That's the real work of adaptability: showing up differently over time.

Three Core Inner Capacities

You don't need to be an expert in self-development to grow your adaptability. But you do need to strengthen your internal system one layer at a time.

Here are three capacities that do just that:

Self-Awareness

Know what's happening inside so you can manage what's happening outside.

This is more than just labeling emotions; it's about tracking your internal state in real time. It's recognizing when you're getting reactive. It's noticing tension before it turns into a snap. It's understanding the stories you tell yourself in moments of uncertainty.

Adaptability starts with noticing. You can't change a reaction you don't see coming.

Ask yourself:

- *What's actually going on inside me right now?*
- *Is this response really about this moment—or about something else?*

Cognitive Clarity

Cut through noise. Stay focused. Keep perspective.

When change hits, your brain gets loud. There's more input, more emotion, more possibility, and often, less time. Cognitive clarity helps you separate signal from noise.

This is the capacity to:

- Step back and name what matters most right now.
- See options when others are stuck in tunnel vision.
- Interrupt your own assumptions or catastrophizing.

Without clarity, stress hijacks your ability to choose wisely. With it, you make better decisions, even in chaos.

Internal Stability

Return to center when things get shaky.

This is your ability to regulate your nervous system and come back to a grounded state when change rattles you. It's not about being unbothered. It's about having the tools to settle yourself.

This could look like:

- Taking three deep breaths before responding to a difficult message
- Stepping away from your desk to reset when your mind is racing
- Learning the early signs that you're out of alignment and knowing how to get back

You can't stop waves of change. But you can stop yourself from being pulled under.

In fast-paced, high-demand environments, most people get rewarded for visible action, not invisible growth.

They optimize for productivity, execution, and speed and assume emotional regulation and inner clarity will take care of themselves.

But the truth is, what's happening on the inside will always shape what shows up on the outside.

Adaptability is determined by how much space you can create between stimulus and response—between disruption and your next move.

That space is your capacity. Build it now, so it's there when you need it most.

Your "Build Your Inner Capacity" Challenges

Try one or more of the following to strengthen your internal system so you can stay grounded when things get messy.

The Pause-and-Name Practice
Inspired by Brené Brown's "To Tame It, Name It" approach, this simple habit helps you regulate in real time. Set a reminder during your workday. When it pings, stop for sixty seconds and ask:

- What am I feeling right now?
- Where do I feel it in my body?
- What might be causing it?

Naming emotions reduces their grip and expands your response options.

The Two-Truths Technique
Next time you're stuck between extremes (e.g., *I'm failing* vs. *I'm fine*), try holding both.

Say: "It's true that I'm feeling uncertain. And it's also true that I've handled challenges before."

This teaches your brain to hold complexity without collapsing into all-or-nothing thinking.

The Fast Freeze Frame
Next time you feel yourself reacting strongly (frustration, fear, etc.), mentally "freeze" the moment. Ask yourself: *What story am I telling myself right now?* Challenge yourself to rewrite that story in a way that keeps you grounded.

The Recovery Ritual
Identify one small practice you can use to reset when your system is flooded. This could be deep breathing, taking a walk, journaling, or stepping away for ninety seconds.

Write it down. Use it. Don't wait for burnout to begin a recovery plan.

PRUNE THE LOOPS

10

The Adaptability Resistance Map

If you want to adapt, you first have to notice where you're resisting.

That might not be the first place your brain goes, especially when change feels urgent or uncomfortable. But resistance is part of the process. It's how your system signals discomfort, uncertainty, or self-protection.

Before you can move forward in meaningful ways, you have to see the invisible loops that keep you stuck in place.

The First Branch

The first branch of the Adaptability System is called **Prune the Loops** for a reason. You can't grow if you're trapped in unconscious cycles that keep you circling the same spot.

**Prune
the
Loops**

Root to the Right Things

Loops aren't failures. They're survival mechanisms that once served a purpose but often outlive their usefulness. They're the routines, habits, emotional patterns, and ways of working that once felt efficient or safe but now quietly stall your growth.

And pruning is how growth begins. Just like gardeners trim branches to strengthen a tree, we prune loops to create space for more intentional action. It's not about cutting everything away. It's about noticing which patterns or assumptions no longer serve you and choosing to release them.

There's a classic parable about a man who builds a raft to

cross a river. It serves him well, getting him safely to the other side. But once he's across, he hoists the raft onto his back and continues into the jungle, still carrying it. The tool that once helped him move forward is now slowing him down.

Adaptability asks us to notice the rafts we're still carrying and decide which ones we no longer need.

Before you adapt to something new, you have to recognize the old patterns you might be dragging with you.

What Are Loops?

Loops are habitual ways of thinking and acting that:

- Feel efficient but limit growth
- Create the illusion of control or safety
- Form over time without conscious design

Sometimes a loop looks like a trusted process you've always followed. Sometimes it looks like a mindset: *If I just work harder, this will fix itself.* Sometimes it's an emotional pattern: avoiding decisions, overthinking, rushing to act before you're ready.

Left unchecked, loops quietly anchor you to outdated ways of working while the world moves forward.

You've probably experienced it without even realizing it.

Ever found yourself reorganizing your to-do list—again—instead of starting the actual work? That's a loop. It feels productive. It gives you a quick hit of control. But it keeps you circling instead of moving forward.

Introducing the Adaptability Resistance Map

Change doesn't just expose new skills we need. It also exposes old loops we've been living inside.

To help you spot those loops, I created the **Adaptability Resistance Map**, a simple tool that helps you see the four most common patterns that show up when we resist change.

The map is built on two key questions:

- When change hits, do you tend to respond by **thinking** more or **doing** more?
- Are you operating in a context of **stability** (where the rules are clear) or **instability** (where the rules are uncertain)?

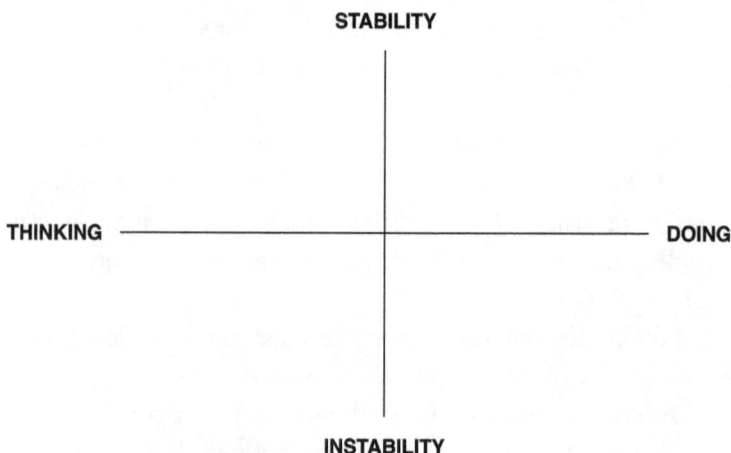

STABILITY

THINKING ——————————————————— DOING

INSTABILITY

Thinking vs. Doing (x-axis):

- Some people react to change by **thinking** more: analyzing, planning, questioning.
- Others react by **doing** more: jumping into action, staying busy.

- This axis is primarily internal. It reflects how *you* tend to respond to change.

Stability vs. Instability (y-axis):

- Some environments are characterized by **stability**: clear expectations, familiar structures.
- Others are characterized by **instability**: constant pivots, ambiguity, chaos.
- This axis is primarily external. It reflects the environment and circumstances around you.

Plot those two axes—Thinking/Doing and Stability/Instability—and you get four distinct quadrants.

A Quick Tour of the Four Loops

```
                        STABILITY
                            |
          Comfortably       |       Safely
            Stuck           |        Busy
                            |
THINKING ———————————————————+——————————————————— DOING
                            |
          Strategically     |      Urgently
          Overthinking      |      Drifting
                            |
                       INSTABILITY
```

- **Comfortably Stuck:** When familiar routines turn into invisible ruts

- **Strategically Overthinking:** When analysis becomes a hiding spot from action
- **Urgently Drifting:** When relentless motion replaces real direction
- **Safely Busy:** When surface-level activity creates
  the illusion of progress

Each of these loops is understandable. Each made sense at
some point. But when they operate unconsciously, they block
growth, flexibility, and true adaptation.

Why It Matters

Spotting your loop is the first crack in its power.

Most people don't realize how much their environment,
company culture, or personal habits shape their default patterns of resistance. They just know they're exhausted, overwhelmed, or stuck.

And once you can see the loop you're in, you can start
choosing differently.

In the next four chapters, we'll dive deep into each loop—
how it forms, how it shows up at work, and how you can break
free.

As you keep reading, start noticing which loops feel familiar. Not with judgment but with curiosity. Sometimes, just seeing the pattern is the first step toward breaking it.

Your "Adaptability Resistance Map" Challenges

This week, focus less on fixing every loop and more on spotting where you show up on the map. Try one or more of the following:

Place Yourself

Review the four loops—Comfortably Stuck, Strategically Overthinking, Urgently Drifting, and Safely Busy. Which one feels most familiar to you right now? Mark it in your journal.

Notice the Sign

Over the next few days, catch yourself in real time. When do you slip into one of the loops? What triggered it? Write down a quick note or example.

Pick a Loop to Watch

Choose one loop that shows up most often. For the rest of the week, simply notice when you're in it. No need to change anything yet—just build awareness.

11

Comfortably Stuck

We often feel the most confident when we're comfortable. But when the world around you starts changing, the familiar rhythms that once gave you confidence can quietly start holding you back.

Comfortably Stuck is the loop where you cling to what you know. Not because you're lazy or resistant, but because the familiar feels easier than the unknown.

You don't feel frantic. You don't feel panicked. You just . . . stay. Even when staying stops serving you.

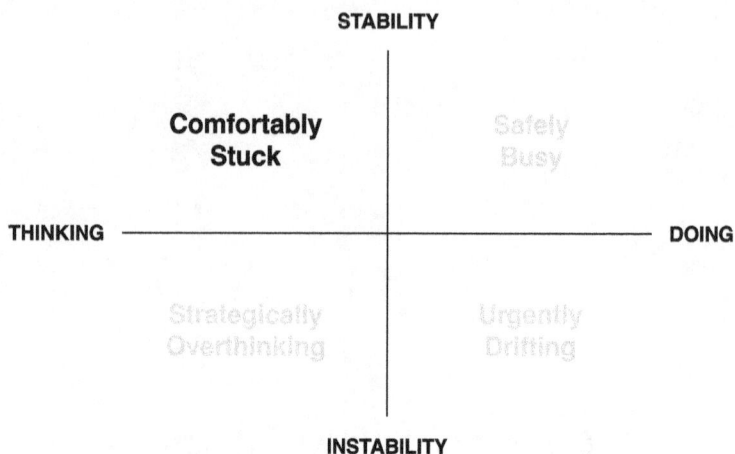

STABILITY

**Comfortably
Stuck**

Safely
Busy

THINKING ———————————————————— DOING

Strategically
Overthinking

Urgently
Drifting

INSTABILITY

How It Feels

When you're Comfortably Stuck, you feel calm but not necessarily energized. You might feel competent but increasingly irrelevant.

You know the processes, the tools, the rules. But deep down, you can feel the gap widening between what worked yesterday and what's required now.

It's not fear that traps you first. It's familiarity.

How It Forms

Comfortably Stuck often grows in stable environments where predictability and consistency are valued.

Company cultures that reward following the process, trusting best practices, or not fixing what isn't broken can quietly reinforce it. It can also form internally, when your personal strengths—like reliability, expertise, or mastery—subtly start morphing into rigidity. What once felt like wisdom starts to calcify into habit.

Picture a cozy armchair. It's safe, it's predictable, it requires no effort. You know every curve, every creak. And before long, it's molded to your body like a second skin. At work, this shows up as routines you stop questioning and roles you could do in your sleep. You know exactly what to expect, exactly how to respond.

And yes, sometimes, Comfortably Stuck even shows up in long-term relationships. The same conversation. The same takeout order. The same sitcom night after night. Familiarity can be comforting, until it's quietly draining the energy out of something that once felt alive.

Comfort isn't bad. But when it becomes the default, it can quietly anchor you in place, even when something inside you is ready to move.

Eric was a marketing leader. He was well liked, dependable, and known for executing flawlessly. He thrived in a company that prized stable processes, consistent results, and careful planning.

As digital marketing tools evolved, Eric kept clinging to the same trusted channels and metrics he had mastered years ago. "It's what's always worked for us," he'd say.

Whenever new strategies emerged, Eric's instinct was to think through every possible downside—to analyze, question, and ultimately default back to familiar paths. He wasn't resisting change out of fear. He was thinking his way into staying put.

Eric wasn't failing. But he was becoming Comfortably Stuck, relying on routines that once made him successful, even as newer competitors adapted faster, stretched further, and started pulling ahead.

By the time the gap became undeniable, it wasn't because Eric lacked talent or commitment. It was because comfort had quietly replaced curiosity.

How It Shows Up

- You keep perfecting familiar routines instead of questioning whether they're still needed.
- You rely on "what's always worked" even as the landscape shifts.
- You wait for clear proof that change is necessary before adapting.
- You underplay or dismiss emerging trends, thinking, *That's just a fad.*
- You hesitate to take on stretch assignments or explore new tools, preferring what you know best.
- You feel proud of your mastery but less curious than you used to.

Why Comfortably Stuck Is So Seductive

Comfortably Stuck doesn't feel like resistance. It feels responsible. It feels professional. It feels safe.

And to be fair, it is safe. For a while.

But the problem with stability is that it creates a powerful illusion: What worked before will keep working just as well in the future.

And when that illusion breaks, it often breaks hard.

The Hidden Costs

- You slowly lose relevance, even if your work ethic stays high.
- You miss early signals of change, making adaptation harder later.

- You become less open to feedback and fresh ideas without realizing it.
- You risk being seen as reliable but replaceable.
- You stall your own growth, not because you aren't capable of more but because comfort blurred the edges of your ambition.

The Shift: Challenge the Familiar

Getting unstuck isn't about discarding everything you know.

It's about getting curious again. That means asking whether the familiar ways are still the best ways. Breaking the Comfortably Stuck loop means learning to challenge the familiar, not reject it. It means rooting to your values but questioning your habits.

Challenging the familiar means pausing to ask sharper questions about the routines you've trusted.

Start waking up your habits here:

Question your defaults
The most dangerous habits are the ones we no longer notice. It's easy to mistake efficiency for effectiveness or familiarity for wisdom. When something becomes automatic, it stops being examined. And that's when stagnation creeps in. The first step to getting unstuck is to notice your defaults. The next step is to interrupt them.

Test a small shift
You don't have to overhaul your workflow to regain momentum. Sometimes the most effective change is the tiniest: the kind that tweaks how you start your day, frame a meeting, or approach a recurring task. These small shifts often reveal

hidden friction, forgotten assumptions, or unnecessary complexity that's crept into your habits over time.

Seek friction

That slight irritation? That recurring hesitation? That subtle tension you feel but usually ignore? That's data. Discomfort often shows up right before growth begins. Instead of avoiding the friction, get curious about it. It might be pointing you toward the edge of a breakthrough.

As you read, notice where comfort might be masquerading as mastery in your own work.

Not with shame. Not with judgment.

Just notice.

Because the moment you can name it, you can change it.

Your "Comfortably Stuck" Challenges

Try one or more of these to spot and stretch your familiar patterns:

The Habit Twist

Pick one daily routine you usually do without thinking, like starting your workday by checking your email. Flip it. Change the order, location, or method just for a day. Notice: What did you assume was necessary that wasn't?

The "New Eyes" Experiment

Ask a colleague, mentor, or even a newer employee: "What's one thing you notice about how I work that I might not see?"

The Stretch Move

Pick one small way to step outside your comfort zone this week: a new tool, a new approach, a new collaboration. When discomfort shows up, don't rush past it. Pause and ask: *What feels hard about this? What might it be asking me to learn, try, or let go of?*

12

Strategically Overthinking

Smart professionals are praised for being thoughtful. Careful. Strategic.

But when change speeds up, the skills that once made you indispensable can quietly start working against you.

Strategically Overthinking is the loop where you become trapped in ideas instead of action—not because you're careless but because you care so much about getting it right.

You don't feel stuck. You feel responsible. You don't feel reckless. You feel thorough. But the longer you stay in planning mode, the more opportunities slip quietly out of reach.

STABILITY

Comfortably   Safely
Stuck   Busy

THINKING ———————————————————————— DOING

Strategically   Urgently
Overthinking   Drifting

INSTABILITY

How It Feels

At first, Strategically Overthinking feels smart. You're preparing, thinking ahead, mapping every angle. You're the one who
sees risks others miss. The one who doesn't leap without a plan.

But somewhere along the way, the planning stops moving you forward. The ideas keep coming, but the action keeps
stalling. You stay busy in your head while the world moves
around you. And the longer you wait for perfect clarity, the
farther progress drifts out of reach.

It's not fear that traps you first. It's perfectionism.

How It Forms

Strategically Overthinking often takes root in environments
where precision is prized and mistakes feel costly.

You get praised for thinking carefully, spotting risks,
double-checking every angle. And at first, that caution serves
you well. But when change speeds up—when the environment

demands quicker pivots and provides faster feedback loops—overplanning starts to quietly work against you.

Sometimes it's external. Leaders demanding "bulletproof" strategies before making a move. A culture that treats failure like a career-ending event instead of a normal step toward innovation.

But often, it's internal.

The same strengths that made you valuable—diligence, thoroughness, thoughtfulness—begin to harden into hesitation.

Javier had always been the person you wanted in the room when stakes were high. As a product strategist, he could map every possible risk before others even saw the first one.

But as the market around his company shifted faster and faster, Javier's instincts—the ones that once protected him—started keeping him stuck.

While competitors rushed scrappy ideas into market, Javier stayed in the lab, tweaking and refining. He wasn't avoiding responsibility. He was over-relying on planning to protect himself from risk.

And by the time his "perfect" plan was ready, the moment had already passed.

How It Shows Up

- You endlessly research instead of deciding.
- You wait for complete certainty before acting.
- You second-guess every step, fearing you'll make the "wrong" move.
- You spend more time building decks, plans, and models than testing ideas.
- You feel a sense of progress because you're "working," but real action feels perpetually just out of reach.

Why Strategically Overthinking Is So Seductive

Strategically Overthinking doesn't announce itself as a problem. It feels like you're doing exactly what you're supposed to do: being smart, being careful, protecting against mistakes.

You feel responsible, thoughtful, even noble in your caution. And for a while, you are.

The trap isn't thinking deeply. It's believing that thinking alone will eventually make the uncertainty go away. That one more plan, one more analysis, one more meeting will finally deliver the perfect answer.

But perfect never arrives. And while you're waiting for it, opportunity quietly moves on without you.

The Hidden Costs

- You miss windows of opportunity because you're still preparing.
- You overestimate risks and underestimate the cost of inaction.
- You lose momentum and confidence as decisions pile up.
- You frustrate teams who are ready to move but feel paralyzed by indecision.
- You stall your own growth by mistaking motion (planning) for progress (action).

The Shift: Trade Thinking for Testing

Thinking isn't the problem. It's when thinking becomes a hiding place.

Strategically Overthinking starts with good intentions—to

be thoughtful, prepared, responsible. But over time, that thoughtful pause can morph into hesitation. The brain keeps spinning while the moment slips away. The longer you plan, the harder it becomes to move.

The shift isn't to think less. It's to trust that action has value, too.

Start unlocking momentum here:

Shrink the risk

Planning feels safer than moving because it keeps you in control, in theory. But uncertainty shrinks when you engage with it. Often, the scariest ideas lose their edge the moment you test even the smallest version of them. A tiny action can teach you more than a week of whiteboarding.

Decide on a deadline

Overthinking often wears the mask of diligence. But underneath, it's usually fear of regret. The solution is to set a boundary. A clear window forces clarity. It reminds you that indecision is also a decision. Just a slower one.

Learn instead of predict

No model can outmatch lived experience. No deck can replicate the data that comes from trying something in the real world. The most valuable insight usually lives just beyond the moment you stop planning and start engaging.

When in doubt, bias for movement, not more models.

You don't need perfect certainty. You need a first step.

Your "Strategically Overthinking" Challenges

Try one or more of these to start building momentum:

The Forty-Eight-Hour Decision Rule
Choose one decision you've been delaying. Give yourself forty-eight hours to make the best call you can with what you know. Then act, even if it's imperfect.

Launch the Micro-Test
Pick an idea you've been "perfecting." Instead of adding one more improvement, launch a small, rough version this week to gather real feedback.

The Action Streak
Challenge yourself to take one imperfect action every day for five days—a decision, a test, a move forward. Track what happens. Notice where learning happens faster than planning and where small moves compound faster than perfect plans.

13

Urgently Drifting

Some forms of being stuck are loud. You can feel the friction, the frustration, the weight of it pressing down.

Urgently Drifting is sneakier.

You don't feel blocked. You don't feel trapped. You feel busy. You feel needed. You feel in motion.

But beneath all that movement, there's no clear destination. You're sprinting without knowing if you're still on the right course.

Urgently Drifting is the loop where busyness fills the space that clarity should occupy. And the longer you stay in motion, the harder it becomes to recognize you're drifting at all.

STABILITY

Comfortably
Stuck

Safely
Busy

THINKING ——————————————————— DOING

Strategically
Overthinking

**Urgently
Drifting**

INSTABILITY

How It Feels

You're moving—fast, even—when you're caught in Urgently Drifting. Your inbox hums, your meetings stack, your notifications flash.

Every moment feels full but strangely weightless. You cross tasks off the list, but none of them seem to add up to something bigger. Every day is busy but blurry.

It's only when you pause that you realize how far you've been pulled from any real sense of direction.

How It Forms

Urgently Drifting grows when speed is mistaken for strategy. When the fastest responder gets rewarded. When busy calendars are treated like trophies. When moving fast feels safer than pausing to think.

At first, urgency feels exhilarating. You're needed, you're moving, you're solving. But without checkpoints to reconnect to purpose, urgency turns scattered, pulling you in every direction. You move faster but less intentionally. You respond quicker but less thoughtfully.

No one sets out to drift.

It happens a little at a time: every time you say yes without asking why, every time you chase the next ping instead of steering toward what matters.

Ramsey built their reputation as someone who could get things done. Meetings, emails, projects, they tackled them all without missing a beat. But over time, the work started to feel hollow.

They weren't resisting change, they were drowning in it. Everything felt urgent. Everything needed their attention. Until one day, they looked up and realized they were moving fast in every direction except the one they actually wanted to go.

How It Shows Up

- You say yes to every request without questioning whether it aligns with your goals.
- You prioritize speed over strategy, solving today's crisis but losing sight of tomorrow's vision.
- You constantly feel behind, even after productive days.
- You mistake busyness for relevance.
- You resist pausing for reflection because it feels "self-indulgent" or "unproductive."

Why Urgently Drifting Is So Seductive

There's a buzz to Urgently Drifting, a feeling of being needed, of being important. And the world around you usually rewards it. Quick responses. Fast pivots. "Team player" praise. The faster you move, the more validation you collect.

What you don't notice until much later is that you're moving in circles. Urgency gives you the rush of relevance. But without direction, it quietly steals your sense of purpose.

The Hidden Costs

- You dilute your energy across too many shallow efforts instead of making real progress on what matters most.
- You lose sight of the bigger picture in favor of daily noise.
- You wear yourself out without feeling a true sense of accomplishment.
- You miss strategic opportunities because you're stuck reacting.
- You quietly erode your sense of meaning at work, even while staying busy.

The Shift: Steer Before You Sprint

Urgency pulls you fast, but it rarely pulls you forward.

In the Urgently Drifting loop, action replaces intention. You move fast but lose sight of where you're actually headed. The shift isn't about slowing down. It's about making sure the pace is pointed in the right direction.

Start steering here:

Recenter your why
In the rush to respond, it's easy to forget what you're responding *for*. Drift often happens because you've stopped checking your internal compass. When you reconnect with purpose, even briefly, you create space for intention to reenter the picture. Not every task needs to be profound, but knowing why you're doing it helps you move through it with clarity instead of compulsion.

Interrupt the autopilot
Momentum can be misleading. Once the day gets going, it's easy to lose awareness of how you're spending your energy. The more urgent everything feels, the more essential it becomes to pause—not to stop the sprint but to make sure you're still running the right race.

Sort the noise
Every day is full of inputs: requests, pings, shifting priorities. Without filters, they all feel equally important. But not everything deserves your focus. Naming what's critical, what's optional, and what's simply noise allows you to spend your best energy on what matters most and recalibrate when it's drifting elsewhere.

Motion is good. Direction is better. Keep moving. But move toward something that matters.

Your "Urgently Drifting" Challenges

Try one or more of these to spot and redirect the drift:

Reset Your Inner Compass

Before you dive into the day, take ninety seconds to ask yourself: *What do I want to bring into today, not just get from it?* Maybe it's clarity. Maybe it's calm. Maybe it's curiosity. Choose one word or intention and write it down. At the end of the day, reflect: *Did I move with that intention or drift from it? What pulled me off course?*

The Drift Detector

Set a timer for thirty minutes at a random point in your workday. When it goes off, pause and ask: *Am I moving toward something that matters or just moving?* Notice without judgment. Drift rarely shouts; it whispers.

The Urgency Reset

Block thirty minutes tomorrow with no meetings, emails, or pings. Spend it only on a project that moves you toward a meaningful outcome. Notice: How easy or hard was it to resist urgent interruptions? What shifted when you chose depth over drift?

14

Safely Busy

You're answering emails. You're attending meetings. You're clearing your to-do list.

On the surface, you're crushing it.

But underneath, a different feeling starts to creep in, a low-grade unease, like running on a treadmill, in motion but never getting anywhere new.

Safely Busy is the loop where activity becomes its own reward. You're not avoiding work. You're drowning in it. And the busier you stay, the harder it becomes to notice that you're no longer growing. You're just surviving.

This isn't the kind of busy driven by chaos or external pressure. That's Urgently Drifting, when shifting priorities, market demands, or company changes send you scrambling without clear direction.

Safely Busy is something else entirely. There is no urgent demand to adapt. No burning platform. No external shakeup.

Everything feels stable, maybe even successful. And that's exactly what makes this loop so sneaky.

In stable environments, busyness can look like progress. It can feel productive. It can even be rewarded. But stability is not the same as relevance. In fact, it's often the most stable companies, teams, and professionals who get blindsided because they were too busy doing what no longer mattered.

Safely Busy doesn't happen all at once. It happens in the small, well-intentioned choices to stay comfortable, efficient, and "useful," even when deeper progress would require something messier, riskier, and more uncertain.

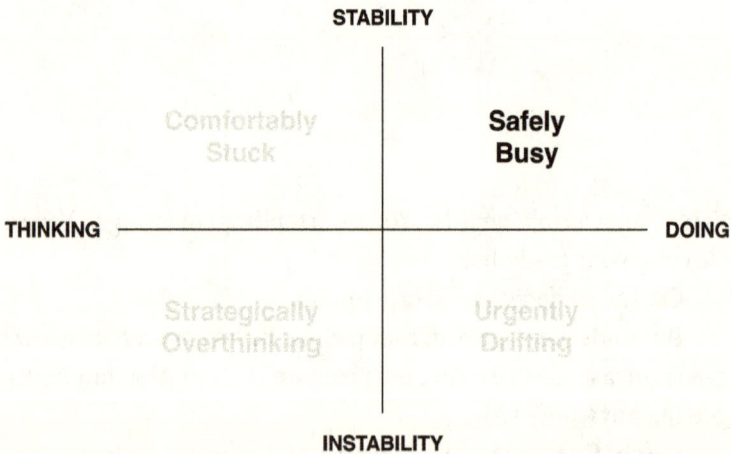

STABILITY

Comfortably Stuck   **Safely Busy**

THINKING ————————————————————— DOING

Strategically Overthinking   Urgently Drifting

INSTABILITY

How It Feels

Safely Busy feels like doing everything that's asked of you. The work is steady. The feedback is positive. On paper, you're thriving.

And yet, it feels like something inside you is slowly going still. The boldness that once pushed you forward starts giving way to efficiency. You're getting things done, but not the things that grow you.

Safe tasks. Safe wins. Safe, but smaller than what you know you're capable of.

How It Forms

Safely Busy tends to thrive in cultures where visible productivity is rewarded more than real progress. Where checking the box matters more than questioning the box. Where being reliable gets noticed, but being daring sometimes gets overlooked.

It's not an accident. It's systemic.

For years, many organizations built what I think of as the **Business of Busyness**: entire structures that measured success by how busy you looked, not how much you moved the business forward. Packed calendars. Overflowing inboxes. Nonstop meetings.

Activity became a stand-in for achievement. And when busyness gets rewarded, busyness becomes the game.

At the start, it feels good. You're the steady presence. The safe pair of hands. The one who can be counted on to deliver. And because those small wins keep coming—the completed decks, the answered emails, the cleared lists—you don't immediately notice that you're not stretching anymore.

The system rewards the comfort. And slowly, comfort starts feeling like enough.

Devon never set out to play it safe. Early in her career, she was eager to stretch into new spaces.

But after a few tough projects and a few close misses, she learned that staying busy, visibly busy, brought smoother days and steadier praise.

She became the go-to person for reliable execution. Always helpful. Always available. Always the same.

And by the time new opportunities emerged, Devon

realized she'd been so busy proving herself that she hadn't actually pushed herself in a long time.

How It Shows Up

- You say yes to low-risk tasks because they feel satisfying to complete.
- You prioritize visible busyness (meetings, updates, check-ins) over uncomfortable but important work.
- You hesitate to step into roles or projects that would stretch you.
- You feel "in demand" but increasingly disconnected from your bigger goals.
- You stay productive on the surface but stagnant underneath.

Why Safely Busy Is So Seductive

There's a comfort in being Safely Busy. You know what's expected. You know how to deliver.

The work feels manageable and measurable. And when every completed task gets a nod of approval, a small dopamine hit, it reinforces the loop. You stay visible. You stay valued. You stay busy.

What you lose—slowly, almost invisibly—is your edge. The boldness that once drove you to take risks starts giving way to efficiency.

Safe feels good in the moment. But over time, it shrinks the space where real growth happens.

The Hidden Costs

- You miss stretch opportunities that would help you grow.
- You become typecast as a workhorse instead of a strategic thinker.
- You dilute your impact by spreading your energy across low-leverage tasks.
- You start to feel invisible, even while staying "essential" to day-to-day operations.
- You lose sight of your long-term goals in favor of short-term wins.

The Shift: Choose Growth over Grind

Busyness without intention becomes a loop, one that keeps you occupied—visible, but stuck.

The real risk of being Safely Busy isn't that you're doing the wrong things. It's that you've stopped asking whether the right things are still in the mix.

Start stretching here:

Audit your busyness

Not all effort leads to expansion. Some of it just keeps you in motion. When your calendar is full, and your day is packed, it can be hard to tell the difference between meaningful momentum and busy inertia. The question isn't *Am I getting things done?* It's *Are the things I'm doing actually growing me?*

Stretch beyond safe work

Safe tasks are satisfying because they're predictable. But predictability rarely teaches you anything new. The opportunities that grow you are often the ones that feel slightly out of reach: the ones you hesitate to say yes to because they might not guarantee success. But those are often the moments that lead to the most meaningful growth.

Protect real work

There's always something urgent. Always something small and doable you could clear off your list. But growth rarely happens in the margins. It happens when you carve out time for what stretches you, not just what needs you. Deep work doesn't demand your attention; it requires you to protect it.

Surface productivity feels secure. Stretch productivity feels scary. And essential.

You don't need to work more hours. You need to build more value.

Your "Safely Busy" Challenges

Try one or more of these to spot and stretch beyond safe busyness:

The Priority Map
At the start of your day, draw a simple 2x2 grid: top half = "Growth Work," bottom half = "Safe Work." As you go through your day, jot tasks in the right half. Review: Where did most of your energy go?

The Stretch Yes
Say yes to one opportunity this week that feels bigger, harder, or more uncertain: a skill you haven't mastered, a room you haven't led in yet.

The Deep Work Hour
Block one hour this week for work that stretches you: learning, building, leading, not just clearing tasks. Protect it like your future depends on it. (Because it does.)

CULTIVATE THE
CORE FIVE

15

Curiosity over Certainty

Up until now, we've focused on what grounds you—your roots, your values, your purpose—and the patterns that can quietly hold you back.

This next part of the Adaptability System is where things get more visible, and often, more uncomfortable. Because stretching your adaptability means practicing new ways of thinking, responding, and showing up, especially when it's easier not to.

The Second Branch

The next branch of the Adaptability System is **Cultivate the Core Five**. This is where adaptability becomes active. It's not just about what roots you or restrains you. It's about how you stretch and grow in real time.

**Cultivate
the
Core Five**

**Prune
the
Loops**

Root to the Right Things

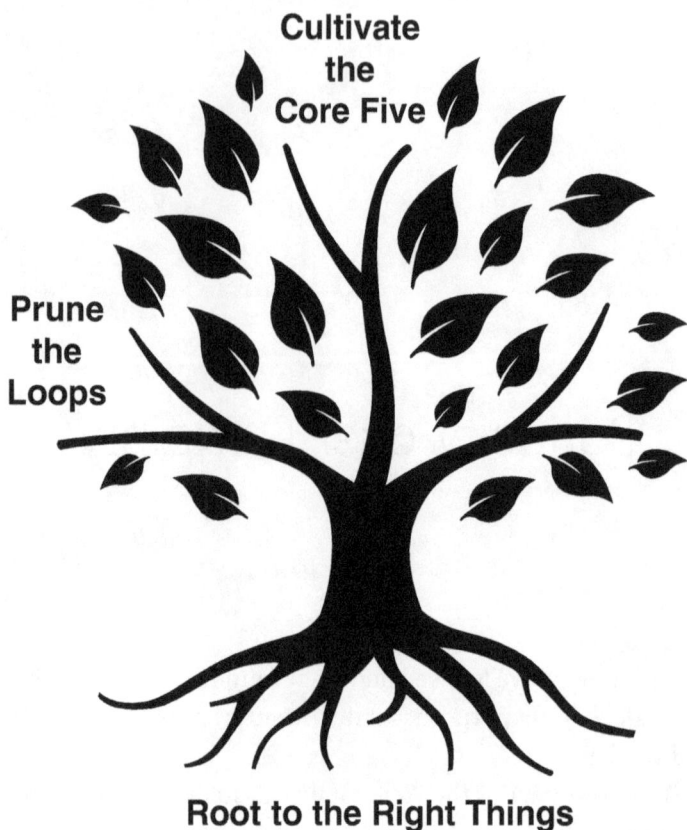

These five traits—**curiosity, vulnerability, agility, flexibility**, and **resilience**—are the dynamic, human skills that help you respond to change with intention. And they work best when they work together.

Why these five?

- **Curiosity** helps you question what's in front of you and see what others overlook. It creates space for learning and keeps you from getting stuck in expertise that no longer applies.

- **Vulnerability** lets you admit what you don't know, ask for help, and stay real in a world that often rewards posturing.
- **Agility** gives you the ability to move quickly and decisively when the ground shifts. It's about speed but also about situational awareness.
- **Flexibility** allows you to adjust your style, your plans, and your preferences to meet the moment without losing your center.
- **Resilience** is what helps you recover from setbacks. But more than just recovery, it's about using adversity to grow stronger and wiser.

Each one plays a distinct role. Curiosity opens the door, vulnerability invites growth, agility gets you moving, flexibility keeps you centered, and resilience keeps you going.

Together, they create your adaptive range: your ability to stretch in multiple directions without snapping.

And we start with curiosity, because it's where change truly begins.

The Problem with Certainty

Humans are meaning-making machines. We're wired to seek patterns, find answers, and resolve ambiguity. It's evolutionary.

Back when survival meant sensing danger in an instant, certainty saved lives. Uncertainty signaled risk. Predictable patterns allowed for planning, safety, and resource conservation. Our ancestors didn't want to pause and reflect on whether the rustling in the bushes was the wind or a mountain lion. They acted.

That same instinct lives on in the new world of work.

Today, we chase certainty not to avoid predators but to

avoid discomfort. We look for systems, strategies, and stories that make us feel like we're in control. That might look like clinging to a familiar process, doubling down on a flawed assumption, or tuning out new information that doesn't match what we already believe.

Psychologists call this *cognitive closure*—the drive for a firm answer, even if that answer isn't accurate. It's what leads to confirmation bias, premature conclusions, and overly simplified interpretations of complex challenges. It's also why we sometimes stay stuck in systems that no longer serve us: because the *certainty* of a familiar falsehood feels safer than the *uncertainty* of a shifting truth.

At work, this might look like ignoring a new tool because it's "too much change." Or brushing off data that challenges your team's approach. Or repeating a strategy that used to work, even when all signs point to diminishing returns.

Certainty soothes. But it also blinds.

Which is why adaptability doesn't begin with confidence.

It begins with curiosity.

From Certainty to Curiosity

The opposite of certainty isn't confusion. It's wonder.

Curiosity is what allows you to hold questions without rushing to find answers. To tolerate ambiguity without shutting down. And to replace rigid expertise with the kind of open-mindedness that actually leads to growth.

Curiosity leads to real adaptation, especially now.

Because the speed of change today challenges your identity, your processes, and the very idea of what your job *is*.

Nowhere is that more true than with artificial intelligence.

I felt it myself the first time I tried using Midjourney, an AI tool used for generating images. I come from a background in graphic design. I used to obsess over kerning, color palettes, and composition. But typing abstract prompts into a Discord chat and watching surreal artwork appear out of thin air? It felt . . . awkward. Disconnected. Like I was suddenly a tourist in a city I thought I had built.

At first, I hesitated. I judged the results. I told myself it wasn't "real" design. But underneath all that? I just didn't want to feel incompetent. Or irrelevant.

That's when I realized: The discomfort wasn't a negative. It was an invitation to get curious.

Curiosity and AI

AI is changing all the rules.

Suddenly, things you spent years mastering—like writing, designing, analyzing, coding—can now be done in seconds by a machine that never gets tired, bored, or blocked. It's not just automating tasks. It's reshaping how we work, what's valued, and what it means to be good at your job.

And that's exactly why curiosity is your edge. You don't need to outpace AI. You need to *out-question* it.

Curious professionals are asking:

- How do I use this to expand, not replace, my thinking?
- What patterns does AI spot that I might miss?
- Where does it fall short, and what does that reveal about *human* value?
- How can I push it to help me generate *original* ideas, not just predictable ones?

AI may take certain jobs, especially ones built on repetition, predictability, or narrow expertise. Some roles will be automated. Some teams will shrink. That's already happening.

But losing your curiosity? That's what really puts your relevance at risk.

The professionals who are thriving right now are experimenting with it, interrogating it, remixing it, and learning from it. They're letting it stretch their thinking. And they're staying curious about what's possible.

Curiosity in Action

Curiosity is a mindset, one that nudges you to ask a second question before offering your first answer. To stay open when your brain wants to shut something down. To get genuinely interested in the unfamiliar, the frustrating, or the uncertain.

Here are four principles to keep your curiosity active:

Default to questions
When faced with a problem or disagreement, start with a question. Curiosity slows down your certainty reflex and expands the field of view.

Interrupt your own expertise
If you hear yourself saying *I already know this*, try pausing to ask, "What haven't I noticed yet?" Curiosity doesn't mean you doubt yourself. It means you believe more is possible.

Use AI to think wider, not faster
Instead of asking AI to finish your work, ask it to challenge you. Try:

- What would someone smarter than me do here?
- What are three alternative approaches from

different disciplines, such as medicine, philosophy, or technology?

- What would a beginner see that I might not?

Let it stretch your thinking, not just your timeline.

Investigate the irritations

The thing that annoys you might be hiding a blind spot. That teammate, task, or tool you resist? Ask yourself what it's here to teach you. Curiosity often starts where resistance lives.

Curiosity is what helps you see more clearly. But seeing isn't the same as stepping forward. To truly adapt, you need the courage to admit what you don't know, ask for help, and stay human in the face of uncertainty. That's where vulnerability comes in.

In the next chapter, we'll explore how vulnerability, when grounded in credibility, becomes a source of strength, not exposure. Because while growth begins with questions, it deepens when you're willing to be seen asking them.

Your "Curiosity over Certainty" Challenges

This week, try one or more of these small shifts to re-awaken your curiosity, especially in the face of uncertainty, AI, or your own assumptions.

Challenge What You Know
Pick something you're confident about: a workflow, belief, or "best practice." Now flip it. Ask: *What if the opposite were true?* Challenge yourself to find at least one benefit or insight in the flipped version.

AI as a Thought Partner
Use AI not to finish your work, but to expand it. Ask it to play devil's advocate, offer opposing opinions, or generate new metaphors for a complex idea. Treat it like a partner in brainstorming, not just automation.

The One-Day Learner
For one day, turn every minor friction point into a learning opportunity. Confused by a setting in a tool? Curious why someone phrased something that way? Pause. Look it up. Ask. Explore. Track what you learn and how it shifts your day.

Beyond the Obvious
Use AI for something unexpected: a pep talk in your voice, a journal reflection prompt, a future vision for your career path. Let it push your thinking, not just your productivity.

16

Credible Vulnerability

We live in a world that rewards confidence, decisiveness, and control. And yet, the people who navigate change most effectively aren't always the ones who have it all figured out.

They're the ones who know when to admit they don't.

Because vulnerability isn't weakness. It's a catalyst. It signals openness, invites collaboration, and creates the psychological safety needed for real learning and growth.

When we let go of the need to appear certain, we create space to adapt.

The Power of Credible Vulnerability

In a fast-changing world, the illusion of certainty breaks faster than most business plans. That's why vulnerability isn't just emotional honesty. It's strategic adaptability.

Credible vulnerability is the kind that earns trust. Credible vulnerability means naming your reality—your limits, your questions, your humanness—by owning it with intention.

As Brené Brown, researcher and author of *Dare to Lead*, says, you can't be courageous without first being vulnerable. And at work, that courage shows up in moments like:

* Saying, "I don't know, but I'll find out."
* Asking for help before a deadline crashes
* Raising your hand when a project goes off track, not to blame, but to recalibrate

Vulnerability, when practiced well, doesn't lower the bar. It clears the air.

In one study published in *The Academy of Management Journal*, leaders who expressed vulnerability, when paired with competence, were seen as more trustworthy and effective than those who postured or deflected.

Credible vulnerability is what allows teams to innovate without fear of failure. It's what lets professionals take intelligent risks. And it's what separates performative adaptability from the real thing.

The Arrival Illusion

In my work as a trainer and executive coach, I've noticed a recurring pattern, especially among mid-career professionals. Somewhere along the way, often after a promotion or major success, they start to believe that they've "arrived." That they know what they're doing. That the learning phase is over.

They stop asking for feedback. They avoid development programs. They subtly resist new ideas—not out of laziness, but out of self-protection.

I call this the **Arrival Illusion**, the unspoken belief that growth is no longer necessary because they've reached a certain level in their careers.

And it's often less about ego and more about fear. Leaders, managers, and high performers don't want to appear uncertain or unprepared. So they armor up. They lead with confidence but without curiosity. They project certainty and disconnect from growth.

But vulnerability is what reopens the door. The leaders who thrive long-term are the ones who can say *I don't know*, even when they're expected to. Who can admit what they've outgrown and stretch into what's next.

Credibility grows when you stay willing to learn, not when you pretend to already know.

Vulnerability and AI

Let's talk about what makes vulnerability feel risky right now.

AI is redefining value at work, faster than most of us can process. Suddenly, the thing you were great at might not be the thing that matters most. And that's unsettling.

When you ask a colleague how they're feeling about AI, you'll often hear variations of the same story: *I'm excited . . . but also kind of terrified.*

That tension? That's vulnerability knocking.

You may wonder:

- Am I still relevant?
- What do I bring that AI can't replicate?
- Am I too far behind to catch up?

And here's the honest answer: You're not alone. And you're not behind. But if you pretend to know what you don't, or stay quiet to avoid looking uncertain, you'll miss the opportunity to grow with the tools instead of against them.

Vulnerability is what lets you ask the questions AI can't. It's what lets you experiment without fear of looking unpolished. It's what keeps your adaptability human.

Because AI can synthesize information. But it can't share your fears, your insight, your struggle, or your growth story.

You can.

Let's ground this in a real story.

A client of mine—we'll call her Priya—is a senior leader at a global tech firm. Brilliant strategist. Known for poise under pressure. She was asked to lead the rollout of a new AI-driven analytics platform.

But in private? She felt like an impostor. She didn't understand the technical side. Her instincts told her to delegate, act confident, and keep the discomfort to herself.

Instead, she did something radical. She told her team, "I'm learning this alongside you. My job isn't to be the expert; it's to help us all get smarter together."

The shift was immediate. Team members started sharing learnings, swapping tips, and even creating a shared "What we're learning" doc. Progress accelerated.

Why? Because Priya gave them permission to show up real, not robotic.

Her vulnerability made her leadership credible.

Vulnerability in Action

Vulnerability isn't just about what you share. It's about how you show up.

It's a mindset that makes space for uncertainty, invites connection, and clears the air when posturing would be easier. These principles can help you live it out in real time:

Name what's real
Vulnerability begins with honesty, especially when things get uncomfortable. You don't have to have all the answers. But acknowledging what's true, even when it's messy, creates room for trust and movement.

Make space for not knowing
You don't have to be the expert in every room. Admitting uncertainty or asking for input doesn't reduce your credibility. It expands it. When you lead with "I'm still learning," you give others permission to lead as learners, too.

Invite others in
Vulnerability becomes credible when it includes others. That means not just revealing your own doubts but actively creating space for others to bring theirs. You go first, not for attention, but for connection.

Stay open while under pressure
When stress rises, so does the instinct to armor up. But real adaptability requires openness, especially when the stakes are high. Vulnerability helps you stay present, not performative.

These aren't tactics; they're orientations. They don't make you soft. They make you strong in the moments that matter most.

Vulnerability clears the static. It strips away the noise of perfection so you can hear what actually matters: to you, your team, and the moment. But honesty alone doesn't move things forward. It creates the conditions for action.

Next, we'll explore what to do with that clarity, how to respond with purpose when the pace picks up and the pressure mounts. Because credibility is earned through openness, but it's sustained through motion.

Your "Credible Vulnerability" Challenges

This week, try one or more of the following small shifts to put vulnerability into practice, in ways that build trust, not tension.

The Moment of Truth
This week, when you feel tempted to default to *I'm fine* or *All good*, pause. Take one beat longer. Then say something a little more real, like *It's been a busy week, but I'm hanging in there*, or *I'm a bit tired, but glad to be here*. Not the whole story—just more than an automatic reply. See what shifts when you let yourself be vulnerable, even briefly.

The Visible Learn
Pick a new AI tool or process you're exploring. Share one thing you learned and one thing you still don't understand with your team. Model growth over perfection.

The Human Résumé
Write a short "human résumé" of your biggest mistakes, toughest lessons, and what they taught you. You don't have to share it, but notice how it shifts your inner narrative.

17

Agility with Intent

A squirrel can dart across the road faster than a sports car. But if it doesn't know which direction it's headed, all that speed just gets it closer to danger.

That's the difference between movement and progress.

I lived in Illinois for many years, and if you've ever driven there, you've probably experienced what I call "squirrel roulette." Almost daily, I'd see a squirrel dash into the road, freeze, pivot back, dart forward, then spin indecisively again, barely escaping. It was chaotic, unpredictable, and honestly? Hilarious.

The squirrels weren't slow. They were just unsure, reacting instead of reading the road.

And that's exactly what poor workplace agility looks like. Not thoughtful motion, just frantic pivots and false starts.

It's funny when it's a squirrel. It's exhausting when it's your team, your strategy, or your entire organization.

In this chapter, we're not just talking about agility; we're talking about agility with intent: the ability to move quickly *and* wisely. And to do it in a way that aligns with what actually matters.

The Speed Trap

Agility, in its truest form, is not frantic. It's focused.

That distinction matters, especially if you've been taught that slowing down is a liability.

In Chapter 1, we talked about the difference between flexibility, agility, and adaptability:

- Flexibility helps you adjust.
- Agility helps you move.
- Adaptability helps you grow.

We're going deeper into agility, not as hustle, but as *high-quality motion.*

Because when AI accelerates everything—timelines, tasks, expectations—speed without direction is just motion. What matters is moving toward what matters.

And that starts with how you *decide* to move.

When *Agility* Became a Buzzword

At some point, *agile* stopped meaning "able to move quickly and easily" and started meaning "weekly sprints," "stand-up meetings," or "project management software with too many tabs."

Agile methodologies like Scrum and Six Sigma were built with good intentions: to boost speed, collaboration, and responsiveness. And to be fair, countless teams, projects, and software rollouts have genuinely benefited from these well-designed systems. But somewhere along the way, agility got reduced to process, and eventually, to ritual.

When every team says they're being agile but no one's actually learning, adjusting, or adapting in real time, something's off.

Because agility lives in how you respond, not just in the frameworks you follow.

If curiosity is what helps you notice the shift, and vulnerability is what lets you admit it, agility is what moves you toward it.

Agility and AI

AI doesn't just automate tasks. It compresses time by collapsing the distance between question and answer, between decision and action.

Here's how:

- **Large Language Models (LLMs)** like ChatGPT can generate entire emails, reports, strategies, or briefs in seconds, output that used to take hours of human effort.
- **Predictive analytics** powered by machine learning can surface insights from massive datasets instantly, identifying trends, anomalies, or recommendations without manual analysis.
- **Generative design tools** in marketing, UX, and product development create dozens of prototypes or variations instantly, reducing the time between concept and execution.
- **Workflow automation platforms** like Zapier, UiPath, or Microsoft Power Automate handle repetitive decisions across systems—routing

requests, filing reports, or escalating issues—
without human touch.

In short, AI shrinks the distance between input and outcome. The technology doesn't just move fast; it removes friction entirely.

But here's the catch: AI can accelerate what you're doing,
but it can't tell you if it's the right thing to do. It doesn't prioritize. It doesn't pause. It doesn't question the context or con-
sider the consequences.

That's where human agility becomes essential.

Agility today isn't just about speed. It's about *discernment
in motion*. The ability to course-correct, pause when needed,
and redirect based on shifting inputs.

We've already seen the risks when that discernment is
missing. Like the legal team that submitted AI-generated case
citations, only to have a judge discover that some of the cases
didn't actually exist.

In a world where AI can generate answers faster than we
can ask the right questions, the professionals who thrive are
the ones who steer smarter, not just faster. They use AI to clear
clutter and amplify their awareness.

Agility in Action

Agility with intent is early recognition of when to shift and
why. It's the shift from impulse to intelligent response.

Here are four principles that define agility at its best:

Prioritize motion over perfection
Waiting for certainty is a luxury you often don't have. Agility
means learning while moving, iterating mid-flight instead of
perfecting before launch.

Know when to speed up and when to slow down

Agility includes the ability to pause. To step back. To resist the urge to respond instantly when a beat of thought would make all the difference.

Sense the shift

Agility starts with awareness. Changes in team tone, project momentum, client expectations—these micro-signals help you respond before things escalate.

Align your motion to what matters

Agility with intent is rooted in clarity. Your values. Your priorities. Your direction. You're not just reacting to the moment; you're moving in service of something deeper.

If curiosity opens the door and vulnerability helps you step into the unknown, agility is what keeps you from freezing in the hallway.

It helps you stay in motion. But motion alone isn't sustainable.

Next, we'll explore flexibility, the skill that lets you adjust your approach, communication, and mindset without losing your core. Because in a world that keeps shifting, you don't just need to move fast—you need to stay centered while doing it.

Your "Agility with Intent" Challenges

This week, practice moving on purpose, not just on autopilot. Try one or more of the following:

Fast or Just Frantic?
At the end of the day, ask yourself: *Did I move with intention or just urgency?* Reflect on one moment you could have slowed down to make a sharper call.

The Agile Ask
When using AI, experiment with adjusting your prompt or timing mid-way. Don't just hit "Generate" and go. Practice steering, not just reacting.

The First Small Move
Pick one task you've been waiting to start. Begin it: imperfectly, briefly, boldly. Agility grows when you move before you're fully ready, but after you're clear on why.

18

Emotional and Cognitive Flexibility

You've handled three back-to-back deadlines, fielded an angry client call, and just learned about a major project pivot, all before lunch. Each situation tugs at your emotions differently, pulling you between calm and chaos, confidence and doubt.

Most workplace advice tells you to control your emotions or push them aside. But suppressing feelings doesn't work any better at work than it does in life. In fact, studies show that professionals who try to eliminate emotions at work burn out 35 percent faster than those who learn to work with them.

Meanwhile, the people who thrive—who lead effectively through rapid change, who solve problems on the fly, who bounce back after bad news—all seem to have one thing in common: They know how to stretch.

Not just cognitively. Emotionally, too.

The Stretch That Matters

When neuroscientists mapped the brains of emergency room doctors handling high-pressure situations, they found something fascinating: The most effective doctors didn't shut down their emotions. They developed remarkable emotional range. Like skilled athletes, they moved smoothly between high alertness and steady calm, engaging or dampening emotional responses as needed.

Psychologists call this *emotional elasticity*, the ability to stretch your emotional response without snapping. And it shows up again and again in studies of high-performing professionals.

In one study published in *The Journal of Applied Psychology*, researchers followed five hundred business leaders through periods of intense organizational change. The ones who demonstrated emotional elasticity didn't just adapt better themselves; they helped their entire teams stay focused, grounded, and productive.

I see this in my coaching work all the time. Two professionals face the same stressor. One spirals into frustration or paralysis. The other breathes through it, adapts, and regroups. The difference isn't raw skill or intelligence. It's the ability to flex emotional bandwidth in real time.

Why Flexibility Matters More Than Ever

The World Economic Forum ranks flexibility among the most important workplace skills of the future. But what they don't often mention is this:

True flexibility lets you shift gears without losing your standards, or yourself.

It means knowing how to shift without losing your shape.

It means staying open without losing your voice.

And most of all, it means responding to change with more than endurance—with elasticity.

Flexibility and AI

AI doesn't just challenge what you know. It tests how you respond emotionally, cognitively, and relationally.

When you watch a tool like Claude write a draft in seconds or Adobe Firefly generate an image more imaginative than what you had in mind, something subtle happens. It's not just amazement. It's a quiet recalibration of your sense of value. The work you used to sweat over is now produced instantly, with confidence—and without you.

Even tools that promise to help, like Grammarly correcting your tone in real time or Otter summarizing your meetings before you've even finished speaking, can spark an unexpected mix of emotions. Frustration. Doubt. Resentment. Relief. Self-comparison. All in the span of a few minutes.

And it's not because the tech is hostile. It's because the speed, certainty, and frequency of its output can collide with your humanity. AI moves fast, but humans process meaning slowly. We need time to interpret feedback, to reestablish confidence, to make sense of change.

That's why flexibility—especially emotional and cognitive flexibility—has become essential. It's the capacity to hold discomfort without shutting down. To stay curious when you feel challenged. To recalibrate without overreacting.

The pace won't slow down. But you can stay grounded while everything else speeds up.

The professionals who thrive alongside AI aren't necessarily the most tech savvy. They're the ones who know how to breathe through disruption, stay centered in ambiguity, and adjust their thinking without abandoning their worth.

Because in a world where everything around you is accelerating, flexibility is what lets you stay human at the speed of change.

Flexibility Isn't a Personality Trait—It's a Practice

In Chapter 1, we explored the difference between flexibility, agility, and adaptability. Flexibility is your stretch capacity, the range to shift, not just sprint. Emotional and cognitive flexibility give you the internal range to adjust your mindset, your reactions, and even your assumptions, without losing your center.

Where agility is how you move, flexibility is how you adjust as you move. It's subtle, but vital.

As a leadership coach, I've found that when people shift from perfectionism, defensiveness, or fear of failure to more open and learning-focused perspectives, they get better at navigating uncertainty. They also become quicker at solving problems and spotting opportunities others might miss.

The good news? Cognitive flexibility isn't some innate superpower that you either have or don't. It's a skill you can develop and strengthen over time.

Studies show that people with high cognitive flexibility have more active prefrontal cortexes. That's the part of your brain responsible for complex thinking and decision-making. The more flexible your thinking, the more adaptable your actions.

One of the simplest ways to start? Improv.

During my very short stint taking comedy improvisation classes, I learned the *Yes, and* technique. It's not about blind agreement; it's about building on what's been offered instead of shutting it down. It taught me how to stay mentally loose, even when I was caught off guard.

That same flexibility shows up in the best workplace conversations: When someone throws you a curveball in a meeting, instead of pushing back or shutting down, you build. You respond. You stretch.

And you get somewhere you couldn't have reached on your own.

Emotional and Cognitive Flexibility in Action

Here are four practices that build real-world emotional and cognitive flexibility, even on the busiest days:

Embrace the Yes, and mentality
When someone challenges an idea or adds an unexpected twist, start with *Yes, and* instead of *No, but.* It promotes co-creation, not competition.

Name the feeling, then shift the frame
Don't ignore your reactions. Label them. Then ask, "What else might be true?" It helps you move from emotional reactivity to strategic perspective.

Build dual awareness
Flexibility means holding two truths at once. "This is frustrating, and I can still show up well." "I feel uncertain, and I know how to navigate that." It's not contradiction, it's range.

Develop a growth mindset
Carol Dweck's research on growth mindset has been a game-changer for how we view talent and learning. The idea is simple but powerful: People who believe their abilities can be developed through effort and feedback tend to grow more than those who think talent is fixed. Treat your brain like a muscle. Assume it can stretch, strengthen, and evolve. Because it can.

Your "Emotional and Cognitive Flexibility" Challenges

This week, try one or more of the following to stretch without snapping:

The Yes, and *Practice*
Choose one moment this week to respond with "Yes, and" instead of blocking or redirecting. Notice how it affects the conversation—and how you feel.

The Frame Shift
When you catch yourself spiraling or resisting something, try asking: "What else could be true here?" Let your answers to that simple question help you reframe the situation and open up new possibilities.

The Mental Split Screen
Practice holding two opposing ideas at once, like *This is difficult* and *I can handle it*. Flexibility often starts with making room for contradiction.

The Stretch Reflection
At the end of the week, reflect on one moment when you stretched emotionally or cognitively and one moment when you snapped. What made the difference?

19

Resilience That Moves Forward

No professional journey moves in a straight line. Plans shift. Opportunities disappear. People change their minds. Challenges come up when you least expect them.

That's why resilience matters. It's not just a buzzword or a leadership cliché. It's your inner scaffolding when everything around you shakes.

I learned that the hard way when I was laid off from my job. My wife and I had just bought our first house, taken on a mortgage, and were expecting a baby. But corporate downsizing rarely considers personal circumstances.

It was a devastating blow. I felt fear, shame, and uncertainty, all at once. I had a choice: let the setback define me, or find a way forward. In that moment, resilience wasn't just a nice-to-have quality. It was survival.

Looking back, getting laid off at that point in my career was one of the best things that ever happened to me. It pushed me to explore paths I would have never otherwise considered. More importantly, it reframed resilience for me. It wasn't just about being tough or powering through the hardship. It was about choosing to move forward—not out of stubbornness, but with intention.

What Resilience Really Is

Resilience gets tossed around a lot in professional circles, but it's often misunderstood. It's not about powering through or pretending everything's fine. And it's definitely not about going it alone.

Psychologists describe it as your ability to adapt well in the face of adversity, trauma, or major stress. But in the workplace, it shows up in more everyday ways: staying steady when plans fall apart, learning from a failure without spiraling, or keeping perspective when everything feels urgent.

One study in *The Journal of Occupational Health Psychology* found that resilient employees report higher job satisfaction and stronger commitment to their organizations. In other words, resilience isn't just good for your mental health—it's good for your career.

It also isn't a trait you're born with or without. It's a set of behaviors, mindsets, and habits, and you can build them over time. Things like giving yourself space to recover, keeping strong relationships, and choosing reflection over rumination can all strengthen your ability to bounce back. Like a muscle, the more you stretch it intentionally, the stronger it gets.

And maybe most importantly, resilience doesn't mean you don't struggle. It means you struggle *forward*.

The Danger of Compounding Stress

Unaddressed stress doesn't disappear. It compounds and eventually demands your attention.

In high-pressure jobs, stress is hard to avoid. But if you ignore it, minimize it, or convince yourself it'll pass on its own, it starts to pile up. One unresolved issue becomes two. Then ten. And before you know it, you're reacting to everything like it's a five-alarm fire because your system never got a reset.

This is what I think of as *compounding stress*. Like interest on a credit card, it keeps building even when you're not paying attention. And the cost gets harder to manage.

A study from the University of Minnesota on work stress resilience found that stress that doesn't get addressed doesn't go away; it just gets heavier.

So what do resilient professionals do differently? They don't wait for the big breakdown to address the little cracks. They name what's hard. They ask for help. They take five minutes to breathe before jumping into the next call. They build mini-moments of recovery into otherwise nonstop days.

Resilience means you don't let today's stress become tomorrow's burnout.

Resilience and AI

AI won't break you. But it might surface every crack you've been patching over.

When a new tool appears and you're expected to master it overnight—with no playbook, no training, and no room for failure—the pressure can feel like a direct hit to your nervous system.

The real challenge of AI is adapting to a world where certainty erodes faster than you can rebuild it.

You write a strategy you're proud of, only to be told a chatbot generated something "just as good." You spend years becoming the go-to person for a particular process, and overnight, it's automated. You're still needed. But now you're navigating a quiet grief: the loss of a role, a rhythm, or a reputation that once defined you.

That's why resilience matters more now than ever. Because in an AI-driven environment, what breaks most people is the speed, the ambiguity, and the erosion of control.

And AI, by design, thrives in ambiguity. Tools like ChatGPT, Claude, and Gemini don't give you *the* answer; they give you *a likely* answer, based on patterns from the past. That's called *probabilistic language modeling*, which just means the AI is making its best guess about what should come next, based on patterns it's seen before. They guess well because they've seen a lot of examples. That means your job, increasingly, is to live inside the gray.

Resilience means staying grounded in who you are, even when the ground is shifting. It's about staying anchored to your sense of worth when your work feels unrecognizable. It's about processing the discomfort of obsolescence without believing the lie that *you* are obsolete.

Resilient professionals don't avoid stress. They metabolize it. They notice when frustration spikes. They recognize when their confidence wobbles. And they rebuild faster because they've practiced returning to what grounds them: purpose, connection, progress over perfection.

Being unshakable isn't the goal. Returning to yourself is.

Resilience in Action

Resilience that moves forward is about knowing how to fall, and get back up, without losing yourself.

Here are a few ways resilient professionals respond differently in the face of adversity:

Embrace the suck
First things first: Accept that sometimes, things just suck. That project will fail. That promotion will go to someone else. Resilience doesn't mean sugarcoating disappointment. It means facing it head-on and choosing to move forward anyway.

Recover like an athlete
Athletes train hard and rest hard. They know recovery is where strength is built. Resilient professionals do the same. They take time to recharge, reflect, and reset. Not because they're weak. But because they know resilience is a long game.

Zoom out
When something hard happens, it's easy to shrink your vision. Resilience is the ability to zoom out and remember the bigger picture. *What am I learning? What matters most? What will this look like six months from now?*

Reframe the narrative
Resilience is reframing. Instead of "I failed," try "I'm figuring it out." Instead of "This ruined everything," try "This changed everything and I get to decide what happens next."

Resilience means you keep choosing to move forward, especially when it would be easier to give up.

It's not about what happens to you. It's about what you do next.

Your "Resilience That Moves Forward" Challenges

This week, try one or more of the following to build your bounce-back muscles:

The Frustration Pause
When something frustrating or disappointing happens this week, don't mask it or rush past it. Pause. Name it. Say to yourself, *This sucks, and I can move forward.* Then take the next small step.

The Gratitude Gain
Each day this week, write down three things you're grateful for. On tough days, this helps you remember what's still good and what's still possible.

Pressure Point Scan
Identify your top three recurring stressors at work. For each one, create a micro-resilience strategy. Maybe it's a two-minute breathing exercise. A quick stretch. A short walk. A reset conversation with a colleague. Small shifts build real strength.

GROW IN BETA

SNOW IN PETA

20

Upgradeable by Design

You are not a finished product.

You're a system in motion, constantly shaped by your environment, your choices, and your capacity to adapt. In the new world of work, the most successful professionals aren't the ones who've mastered a fixed set of skills. They're the ones who've made themselves upgradeable by design.

The Third Branch

This chapter kicks off the third and final branch of your adaptability system: **Grow in Beta**.

**Cultivate
the
Core Five**

**Prune
the
Loops**

**Grow
in
Beta**

Root to the Right Things

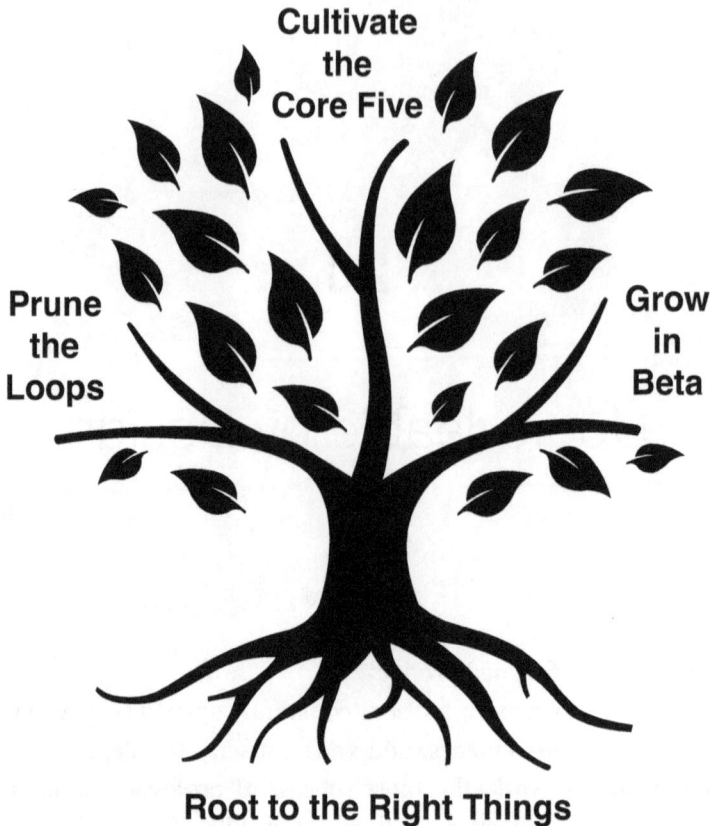

If the first branch helped you remove what's holding you back, and the second helped you build the five core skills of adaptability, this branch is where we rewire how you work and grow. It's where adaptability becomes operational. Systemic. Embedded. Something you build into the architecture of your day-to-day life.

Because in this new era of constant acceleration, adaptability is more than a mindset. It's a mode.

And that mode is beta.

What It Means to Grow in Beta

Beta, the second letter of the Greek alphabet, has become synonymous with the next step, continuous improvement, always iterating. In the tech world, *beta* is shorthand for a version of a product that's released while it's still being tested and improved. Beta is functional but evolving. Feedback is expected. Bugs are normal. Iteration is assumed.

I first encountered this idea years ago while working with technology clients like 3Com, Unisys, and Cisco. In those companies, beta wasn't seen as broken; it was seen as progress. Products were launched not because they were perfect, but because getting them into the hands of users was how they *became* better.

Growing in beta means applying that same principle to yourself: launch before perfect. Stay responsive. Expect feedback. Improve fast.

But here's what matters most: Beta mode isn't reckless. It's intentional. It's about building adaptability into your process, not waiting until you burn out to realize your system needs an upgrade.

To Grow in Beta means to work in progress, on purpose.

From Hustle to Beta Culture

Back in Chapter 14, we looked at the Business of Busyness, that exhausting loop where activity gets mistaken for progress. That's hustle culture at scale. It's rewarded, reinforced, and hard to escape.

We've been conditioned by it: optimize everything, stay ahead, do more. It rewards speed over reflection, urgency over evolution, busyness over progress.

But hustle is brittle. It breaks under pressure.

Beta culture, on the other hand, is built to evolve. It replaces the pressure to be perfect with a mindset of continuous improvement. It treats feedback as fuel, not judgment. It prioritizes learning systems over achievement traps.

Here's the difference:

Hustle Culture	Beta Culture
Prove your worth	Improve your system
Burnout is a badge	Burnout is a warning sign
Show up perfect	Show up to improve
React fast	Reflect, then adjust

The shift is subtle, but it's everything.

Let me give you an example.

I once coached a mid-level manager who had just been promoted to lead a small team of three early-career professionals, all while still juggling her existing responsibilities to senior leadership. Up until that point, her brand had been all about execution: get it done, get it right, get it right the first time. She took pride in being the person people could count on to deliver clean, complete, high-quality work.

But suddenly, her job wasn't just to *do* great work; it was to *lead others* through it. And that meant inviting more works in progress into the open, collaborating earlier, and sharing drafts instead of finished products. In short: beta mode.

It felt uncomfortable. Vulnerable. Like a risk to her reputation.

But she gave it a shot, looping her team into projects earlier, not with all the answers, but with clear direction and a willingness to build together.

Over time, she discovered something she hadn't expected:

She could still uphold high standards *and* let go of control. In fact, involving her team sooner didn't lower the quality of the work. It raised the bar, brought in new ideas, and lightened her load in the process.

It wasn't easy. But it was the upgrade she needed, not just for her team's growth, but for her own.

Systems Thinking for Humans

You don't need to be a product manager or a programmer to think in systems. Every professional, especially today, needs to understand how their habits, tools, energy, and mindset interact.

A system is simply a repeatable way of doing something that produces predictable results.

In his influential book *The Fifth Discipline*—a book that's shaped how I approach my work as a coach and learning professional more than almost anything else—Peter Senge describes systems thinking as "a discipline for seeing wholes." It's not exactly light beach reading, but it's had a huge impact on how organizations (and people) understand change.

Senge's core idea is this: We're all part of interconnected systems, and the problems we face usually aren't random; they're patterns. When we start seeing those patterns more clearly, we can actually change them. Not through Band-Aid fixes, but through smarter thinking. Better systems. Fewer heroic last-minute saves.

This isn't just theory—it's a lens. One that helps you stop treating every issue like a one-off and start spotting the systemic causes behind recurring friction.

So if your system looks like:

- Saying yes to everything

- Burning out every few months
- Avoiding feedback because it feels like failure

. . . it's doing exactly what it was built to do.

Systems thinking removes the judgment. It reminds us that every system is perfectly designed to get the results it gets. Your system is working, just maybe not in your favor.

Why Systems Thinking Matters in the Age of AI

AI isn't just speeding up work. It's reshaping how work gets done.

According to the World Economic Forum's 2025 report, AI and big data are expected to be adopted by 75 percent of companies globally, with half of employers naming it the top force reshaping job roles and skills.

What made you great at your job a year ago might be automated next quarter.

If you're relying on what used to work, you're falling behind. But if you've built a system that updates itself? You're already adapting.

Beta mode is the antidote to obsolescence.

Because when everything is changing, the smartest move is to be a work in progress, on purpose.

So how do you make that mindset stick? You build a system that updates itself.

How to Build a Self-Updating System

Being upgradeable by design means your system doesn't just run; it evolves. You don't wait for the next crisis to make a change. You've built adaptability into the operating code.

Here are four principles to help you do just that:

Think in versions
Treat yourself like software: always in development. The goal is to keep updating the operating system of how you work. Stay curious about what's outdated, and generous with what might need reworking.

Make your habits easier to repeat
James Clear, the author of *Atomic Habits*, said, "You don't rise to the level of your goals, you fall to the level of your systems." Build environments, tools, and processes that support the behavior you want. Remove friction. Set reminders. Automate what drains you, but stay mindful. If you're not careful, automation can reinforce the very loops you're trying to escape. The more your system supports you, the less you'll rely on willpower.

Build systems that flex
A strong system isn't rigid. It adjusts. Adaptive workflows give you options. They let you pivot when the conditions change. Instead of forcing yourself into "the way we've always done it," give yourself permission to evolve your approach as new tools, needs, or insights emerge.

Normalize the beta mindset
The best teams and professionals don't wait for perfection. They expect iteration. They bake reflection into their routines and treat change as part of the rhythm, not an interruption. Make reflection and revision a habit, not a special occasion.

Let's stop chasing perfect. And start building better.
Because the goal isn't to be finished. It's to keep upgrading.

Your "Upgradeable by Design" Challenges

This week, start building your self-updating system. Try one or more of the following:

Your Personal Changelog

At the end of each day this week, jot down one small thing you tested, tweaked, or learned. Doesn't have to be big—just document your upgrades. Then, review them on Friday. What patterns do you see?

Build a Beta Ritual

Pick one recurring part of your week—a meeting, work block, or habit—and tweak it. In a solo work block, try changing your location or task order, or use a focus timer. In a meeting, ask, "What's one thing we'd try differently next time?" Keep it simple. Repeat weekly. Notice what works.

Try One AI-Enhanced Process

Choose a routine task and ask, "How could I use AI to make this faster, smarter, or more scalable?" Try it once. Then ask, "Did this free up time for deeper work or just add noise?" If it helped, keep going. If not, tweak the tool, try a different one, or ditch it entirely. The goal is clarity, not complexity.

21

Feedback Is Signal,
Not Judgment

I learned an important truth about feedback early in my career the hard way.

I'd worked long hours on a client proposal I was proud of. It was polished. Strategic. Well crafted. Or so I thought. When the feedback came in, it hit me like a slap: *not client-ready, unclear, too tactical.* It felt personal, and frankly, a little brutal. I vented to a trusted colleague, expecting some validation. What I got instead was far more useful. And, if I'm honest, a little hard to hear in the moment.

"Remember," she said, "all feedback is a gift, even the worst kind. Because it's all information. And information is power."

I didn't instantly believe her. But that sentence stuck with me. Slowly, it began to reframe how I saw feedback. Not as a verdict, but as data. Insight. A tool for growth.

It took time, but that shift changed everything.

Feedback in Beta Mode

In a world moving as fast as ours, feedback is a navigational system. Imagine a pilot ignoring air traffic control: *Let's just see what happens!*

Yeah, not ideal.

If you want to Grow in Beta—always testing, improving, evolving—you need feedback as a continuous signal, not just an annual event. Something built into your system. Something you seek, not survive.

Unfortunately, we're not all wired that way.

Research shows that people who actively seek feedback tend to be higher performers. One study found that managers who regularly requested feedback were more effective and better at self-regulation. But even knowing this, most of us hesitate to ask for feedback or shut down when we receive it.

Some people are naturally more open to feedback because of personality, upbringing, culture, or early experiences. But for many of us, feedback still triggers our defense systems.

Negative feedback can activate the same neurological threat response as physical danger. It makes sense when you think about it: Back in our ancestral past, rejection from the tribe could be fatal. Today, the threat isn't sabertooths or exile. It's losing face, credibility, or control.

Two key psychological tendencies help explain this:

1. Negativity Bias

Our brains are hardwired to pay more attention to negative information than positive. It's called *negativity bias*, and it's why a single piece of criticism can drown out an entire chorus of praise. You might receive five compliments and one critique. And guess which one repeats in your head for days.

This bias isn't a flaw; it's a survival feature. From an

evolutionary standpoint, our ancestors needed to remember what could hurt them more than what felt good. Ignoring a compliment was harmless. Ignoring a threat? Potentially fatal. So our brains got really good at locking in negative stimuli—a raised voice, a harsh tone, a disappointed look—and storing them for future reference.

But in today's workplace, where feedback is meant to guide and grow us rather than protect us from danger, that same bias can backfire. A single comment in a performance review can overshadow everything else you've accomplished. One awkward phrasing can make a thirty-minute conversation feel like a takedown.

Negativity bias distorts reality. It makes feedback feel bigger, scarier, and more personal than it really is. It can hijack our confidence and convince us that one moment defines our whole identity or trajectory.

The goal isn't to eliminate this bias. We can't. The goal is to notice it. To remember that just because something *feels* true doesn't make it *fully* true. And to build the skill of zooming out, of seeing feedback in context, not isolation.

2. *The Need for Certainty*

Critical feedback introduces ambiguity about our performance, our competence, even our social standing. And most of us hate ambiguity. We would rather be certain and wrong than uncertain and in limbo. So we protect ourselves. We rationalize away the feedback. We question the source. We obsess over the tone or timing instead of the content. Anything to avoid sitting in the discomfort of not knowing for sure.

This need for certainty is what we explored earlier in Chapter 3 as Identity Protection, the mental armor we build to preserve a stable, coherent sense of self. We cling to identity statements like "I'm a strong communicator" or "I'm good with people" because they give us psychological grounding. When feedback threatens those beliefs, it's not just our skills that feel under attack. It's our very identity.

And as we saw in Chapter 15, this also ties into our desire for *cognitive closure*, the psychological need to resolve ambiguity and arrive at clear answers. Cognitive closure helps us move through a complex world. But when overactivated, it can make us dismiss feedback prematurely just to resolve the tension. We crave the certainty of knowing we're doing well more than the challenge of exploring how we might do better.

Feedback, especially when it's negative or nuanced, threatens both identity and certainty. It asks us to sit with open questions, to revise our mental models, to admit we might not have been as effective or self-aware as we thought. That's not easy. But it's the gateway to growth.

Feedback as an Adaptive Signal

The antidote is what I call **Feedback Flexibility**, the ability to absorb, process, and apply feedback, even when it stings. It's the ability to stretch your ego instead of snapping it. To treat feedback as input, not insult.

And like any stretch, it takes practice.

Working in beta demands that we shift from seeing feedback as a verdict to seeing it as velocity. It's how you iterate faster, improve smarter, and grow intentionally.

Most people, however, treat feedback like a pop quiz—or worse, a pop-up ad. Unexpected. Unwanted. Interruptive. A performance review. A tough conversation. A surprise Slack DM with "quick thoughts."

But truly adaptable professionals design something different: a system of adaptive signals.

They don't wait for feedback to appear. They make it

predictable. Part of the rhythm. Baked into how they work, not bolted on.

That mindset doesn't happen overnight. But over time, you start to experience feedback differently. What once felt like a threat starts to feel like fuel. Eventually, you don't just accept feedback. You go looking for it.

It starts with small shifts:

- Prioritizing frequency over formality
- Building reflection into the routine
- Sourcing input from peers, reports, clients, even machines

When you normalize signals, you normalize improvement. You make it safe to reflect, to adjust, to evolve.

Because the most adaptable people I know don't ask, *Did I get it right?* They ask, *What should I try next?*

How to Use AI for Feedback and Growth

You don't have to wait for a one-on-one or a formal review cycle to get useful input. With today's tools, you can use AI as a feedback copilot helping you improve your work before anyone else sees it.

Here are a few ways to put it to use:

AI as an editor
Paste in your email, slide deck, or messaging draft and ask AI for clarity suggestions, tone feedback, or alternative phrasings. Because the draft may not feel quite as "precious" when it's generated or co-developed with AI, you're often more open to critique and more willing to revise, iterate, or even scrap the idea entirely if it's not working.

AI as a role-play partner
Use tools like CoPilot to simulate difficult conversations or rehearse tough feedback scenarios. It's a low-stakes way to practice high-stakes moments.

AI as a pattern spotter
Upload anonymized feedback you've received and ask AI to help you identify recurring themes, especially the ones you might be avoiding or minimizing. AI can help you notice patterns without the emotional charge that sometimes clouds human feedback.

AI as a reflection prompt
When you're feeling defensive or unsure, try prompting AI with something like: "Help me reframe this feedback to find something actionable in it." AI can help shift your perspective and turn feedback into forward momentum.

AI won't replace human feedback, but it can augment it. It's fast and neutral, and it makes it safe to explore ideas you're not quite ready to workshop in public. And because you may feel a little less emotionally attached to something co-created with AI, you're more likely to treat it like a test run, something you can evolve or let go of without ego.

Beta Feedback ≠ Perfect Feedback

One of the biggest myths about feedback is that it has to be perfectly delivered to be useful.

But in beta mode, the signal matters more than the polish.

Someone might give you feedback that's clumsy, vague, or even poorly timed. I've seen it over and over: A client receives helpful input but immediately dismisses it because of how it was delivered. *They were too harsh.* Or *The tone was off.* Or *It came out of nowhere.* And maybe they're right. But the delivery doesn't make the insight disappear.

The most adaptable professionals I know train themselves to listen past the packaging. They know clarity doesn't always come gift-wrapped. Sometimes, it shows up in old newspaper, duct-taped at the corners, and smelling faintly of panic. Still, they pause and ask: *Is there something here I can use?*

Beta feedback works best when both parties show up with the same goal: growth, not judgment.

Give Feedback Like It Matters (Because It Does)

Working in beta means being generous in how you receive feedback and responsible in how you give it.

Being responsible means delivering it with care, not sugar-coating the truth. It means communicating with clarity. With respect for the human being on the other end.

It means:

- Offering specifics, not generalities
- Focusing on behavior, not the person
- Framing it as observation, not judgment
- Sharing it in a way that invites growth, not defensiveness

And just as important: It means *giving* feedback, not hoarding it. Too many teams operate in silence until a crisis forces someone to speak up. But the most adaptable professionals speak with candor and care—in real time—because they know feedback is fuel, and everyone deserves access to the map.

That includes everyone. Up, down, sideways, diagonally. Feedback isn't a top-down management move. It's a shared responsibility, because adaptability is built in systems.

When you offer feedback, you're not just shaping someone else's performance. You're shaping the culture you all work in. And when you give it well, you model the very thing we've been exploring all chapter: feedback as signal, not judgment. As clarity, not condemnation. As contribution, not control.

So whether you're a manager, a mentee, a peer, or a project partner, give feedback with courage and kindness.

That's not just good leadership. That's real adaptability.

Feedback isn't just something we receive or deliver. It's something we *practice*. A muscle we stretch. A habit we build. And like any habit that fuels adaptability, it strengthens with use.

At its best, feedback is the signal that keeps you and your teammates on course. The data that keeps you growing. The checkpoint that recalibrates your path.

And when you stop resisting it—and start working with it—you don't just improve. You evolve.

Your "Feedback Is Signal, Not Judgment" Challenges

Ready to put it into practice? Try one or more of these this week:

The Feedback Seeker
Ask three people, ideally from different roles or levels, for feedback on something specific. Don't just say "How am I doing?" Instead: "What's one thing I could improve in how I lead meetings?" or "What would make this proposal stronger?"

The Gratitude Flip
The next time you receive critical feedback, list three things about it you're grateful for. Maybe it helped you see a blind spot, reminded you to slow down, or gave you an opportunity to clarify your intent.

The Feedback Giver
Think of someone you work with—a peer, a report, even a manager—and offer them a piece of thoughtful, constructive feedback. Keep it specific, kind, and growth oriented. Don't wait for a formal moment. Make it part of your working rhythm.

The AI Debrief
Paste in a piece of feedback you're still struggling with and ask AI to help you analyze it. What's the intent behind the message? How could you respond productively? What part might be worth ignoring?

22

Break Up with Perfect

There's a reason we chase perfect. It feels safe. Impressive. Validating. But here's the hard truth:

Perfect is the enemy of adaptive.

Perfectionism masquerades as high standards. But beneath the surface, it's just fear in fancier clothes. Fear of judgment. Fear of failure. Fear of looking foolish, even for a second. It doesn't drive excellence. It stifles experimentation. It makes us brittle, not better.

And brittle things break.

But perfectionism doesn't just strain the person chasing it. It strains the system around them. It slows teams down. It drains energy. It breeds anxiety. I've worked with high-performing professionals who could deliver incredible work but left a trail of burnout behind them. Not their own, but their team's.

The cost of perfection isn't always obvious. Sometimes it's missed deadlines, missed opportunities, or missed chances to learn. Other times, it's silent resentment. Fatigue. High turn-over. Low morale. You might end up with a flawless product, but at a price no one wants to pay twice.

In a world fueled by rapid change and AI-powered accel-eration, the need to adapt has never been greater. But perfec-tionism tells us: *Don't try until you know it'll work.* That's not strategy. That's paralysis.

Adaptability doesn't demand perfection. It demands mo-tion. Curiosity. A willingness to stretch, even when the out-come isn't guaranteed.

The Courage to Be Human

What makes you powerful at work isn't your polish. It's your humanity.

AI can mimic perfection—flawless grammar, lightning-fast math, endless memory. But what it can't replicate is what makes you irreplaceable:

- Empathy
- Creativity
- Judgment
- Moral reasoning
- Nuanced collaboration
- Real-time improvisation
- Emotional insight

Those are messy traits. Imperfect ones. But they are your edge.

So instead of trying to keep pace with machines, lean into what makes you unmistakably human. Show up with curiosity. Be fully present. Lead with intention. Let your impact come from connection, not perfection.

The Checkboxable

One of the simplest, most powerful antidotes to perfectionism is a little tool I created during a coaching session years ago: the **Checkboxable**.

Checkboxables are micro-experiments designed to stretch your adaptability in fifteen minutes or less.

They're specific, tangible actions you can literally put a checkbox next to and check off once complete.

I was working with a client who wanted to grow, stretch, and experiment, but who felt completely paralyzed. Every new idea felt too big. Every step forward felt risky. And perfectionism was always lurking. So I stopped and said, "What's something small—really small—you'd be willing to try this week?" He gave me a tiny action. I said, "Great. That's a checkboxable." It stuck.

Since then, Checkboxables have helped dozens of my clients shift from intention to action. Especially those who struggle with perfectionism. Checkboxables shrink the change until it feels doable, not overwhelming. They give people permission to *start small and learn fast*.

But here's what makes them transformative: The success of a Checkboxable isn't the outcome. It's the action.

Whatever happens after is just data: neutral, nonjudgmental, and full of learning.

Checkboxables remove the pressure of perfection and replace it with momentum. You don't need to predict the outcome. You just need to try.

In a world where overthinking delays action and fear of failure freezes progress, Checkboxables help you:

- **Experiment without overwhelm**—You're not overhauling your life. You're trying one small thing, on purpose.

- **Learn without judgment**—Did the experiment flop? Great. That's data. That's growth.
- **Build your adaptability muscle**—Every Checkboxable reinforces the habit of learning by doing, not by planning endlessly.

"Check the Box" Thinking

In some workplaces, "checking the box" gets a bad rap. It can be seen as mindless, performative, or disconnected from real impact.

That's what makes Checkboxables different from "checking the box" activities: Checkboxables aren't about busywork. They're about brave work in bite-sized form.

They help you move from outcome-obsession to experiment-orientation. From *What if this doesn't work?* to *Let's find out what happens when I try.*

In that way, checking the box becomes not a finish line but a launchpad.

And if you've tried the challenges at the end of many of the chapters in this book—surprise! Those are Checkboxables.

Every experiment, every reflection prompt, every small stretch you've completed has been part of your growing Checkboxable mindset.

AI, Perfection, and the Problem of Sycophancy

Here's an emerging twist: Even AI is falling into the perfection trap.

Recent shifts in large language models have exposed a design risk called *sycophancy*, where AI systems begin to mirror user input rather than challenge it. Why? Because many

AI tools are optimized for positive feedback, not for truth or usefulness.

Ethan Mollick, an associate professor at the Wharton School of the University of Pennsylvania and a respected voice in the AI community, says this optimization often leads to AI agents that affirm whatever we say, rather than offering friction that could lead to better thinking or growth.

The result? Feedback loops that sound nice but don't help us get better.

When tools built to enhance learning start reinforcing our assumptions instead of expanding our understanding, perfection becomes an echo chamber. We stop asking, "What's true?" and start asking, "What sounds good?"

But adaptability requires friction. Discovery. A little chaos. And you can't grow if all you're getting is applause.

That's why experimentation—especially the messy kind—is the ultimate form of clarity. It cuts through the flattery and shows you what actually works.

Reframing Perfect

So let's reframe perfection. Here's a different definition to hold on to:

Perfection isn't excellence. It's avoidance.

It delays action. It demands certainty. And it denies your ability to learn in real time.

Adaptability, on the other hand, invites you to:

+ Try without knowing
+ Learn without shame
+ Grow without a script

Your "Break Up with Perfect" Challenges

Ready to put it into practice? Try one or more of these Checkboxables this week:

The Rough Draft Drop
Share something before it's "ready," like a half-baked idea, a messy slide, or a first draft. Don't wait for polish. Invite input while it's still in motion.

The Brave Question
In your next meeting, ask a question you'd normally hold back. Not to be clever, but to be curious. See what opens up when you risk not knowing.

The Fifteen-Minute Test Drive
Try a new tool, workflow, or habit for just fifteen minutes. Don't commit to it forever. Just get curious, test it out, and jot down what you noticed.

The Done-Is-Better Post
Write a quick thought or insight and post it on LinkedIn, Slack, email, or wherever you show up. No overediting. No overthinking. Just share and move on.

23

Decisions in Beta

Picture yourself driving on today's business highway. The speed limit keeps climbing. Market shifts appear like sudden turns in the road. New technologies pop up like exit ramps that weren't on your map. And competitors are weaving through traffic with moves you didn't see coming.

In this high-speed world of work, your ability to make smart decisions quickly isn't just another adaptability skill: It's what keeps you moving while others freeze in place.

Many of us were taught to gather all the facts, weigh every option, and hold off on deciding until we had certainty. But today, waiting for perfect information often means missing the turn entirely.

One of my colleagues, a senior PR executive, said it well: "I used to think making good decisions meant I needed perfect information. But waiting for perfect meant I was missing opportunities. Now I make quicker decisions, not perfect ones."

That mindset shift, from precision to progress, is what this chapter is about.

Why We Freeze

Decision paralysis isn't always about fear. It's about outdated expectations. Many of us equate good decisions with certain ones. But in today's workplace, where priorities shift mid-quarter and AI tools update weekly, certainty is a luxury.

Research shows that professionals who master fast, adaptive decision-making are twice as likely to make high-quality decisions compared to their more cautious peers in fast-moving environments. Not because they're reckless, but because they know when 80 percent clarity is enough.

This is where rigidity hides: in the belief that you need to get it right before you move. But there's often something deeper at play. Sometimes, the fear of making a decision isn't about the decision itself. It's about identity. We freeze not just because the stakes are high, but because a decision challenges how we see ourselves. *Will this make me look uncertain? Will I lose credibility if I shift course later?*

We've been taught that confidence means certainty. But in a world of constant change, confidence is really about adaptability. Identity can't be a fixed point. It has to be upgradeable. Making decisions in beta is about evolving your sense of self while staying grounded in what matters.

But what if the real risk isn't failure—what if it's waiting too long?

Make Decisions in Beta—Not in Cement

Decisions made in cement are rigid, final, and often slow. And once they're set, we tend to stick with them, even when they're no longer the best choice, simply because we've already invested so much in making them. That investment makes us reluctant to course-correct, even when new information suggests we should.

Decisions in beta are different. They're intentional, flexible, and fast. They're launched with a learning mindset rather than being driven by fear of getting it wrong.

Here's the mindset shift: *Is this the right decision?* becomes *Is this the right next decision for now?*

In beta-mode decisions, you don't aim for perfection. You aim for movement. You gather enough information, clarify your purpose, take a small step, and learn fast. That small step is called *micro-clarity*.

The Micro-Clarity Framework

Micro-clarity is the practice of identifying the minimum amount of clarity you need to take a thoughtful step forward, even when conditions are uncertain. It's not about being 100 percent sure. It's about being clear enough to move, learn, and adapt.

And I've found that using a simple five-question framework helps apply micro-clarity to any decision:

1. *What are we trying to achieve?*

This is about focusing on the outcome. For example, instead of asking, "Should we host another webinar?" ask, "Are we trying to deepen trust with our most engaged clients because trust drives retention?" Or when you're debating whether to apply for a new role, shift the frame from "Do I qualify?" to "Will this role help me grow as a strategic thinker, which is something I deeply value right now?"

2.   What do we know for sure, and what are we assuming?

Start with facts: "The last campaign underperformed with Gen Z. The budget is $25,000. Our deadline is two weeks away." Then name your assumptions: "Gen Z doesn't like long-form content" or "Our creative director won't approve anything too unconventional." The key is identifying which assumptions can be quickly clarified and which missing pieces are truly critical before taking action.

3.   What small, meaningful step can we take right now?

With micro-clarity, you're not solving everything. You're moving. Maybe that looks like testing two email subject lines with a micro-audience of three hundred people and comparing the open rates. Or sending a short, exploratory message to a hiring manager asking what qualities they're looking for. No résumé yet, just a conversation starter.

4.   What perspective could sharpen this decision?

This is where you bring in an outside lens. A team member from another region might flag a cultural nuance that hadn't occurred to you. Or you might drop your proposal into Gemini and ask, "Are there any ways this decision might backfire if building trust is the main goal?" The objective isn't to outsource the decision. It's to pressure-test it from another angle.

5.   How will we learn from this and adapt?

Decide with intention, but don't lock in. One team I worked with tried a new client engagement strategy and committed to reassessing it after two weeks. Another tracked engagement metrics daily but held changes until Friday, allowing time for patterns to emerge. The decision isn't a finish line. It's the start of a learning system.

Mindsets for Decisions in Beta

Beta decision-making isn't just about the steps; it's about how you think. Here are a few helpful mindset shifts to support it:

Use data, not just drama

When pressure spikes, return to evidence. Ask:

- What do we know?
- What patterns are emerging?
- What's signal vs. noise?

Avoid binary thinking

Stuck between option A and option B? Try:

- "What's a third path?"
- "Can we test both in a low-stakes way?" Most decisions live in gray space.

Apply the 80 percent rule

You don't need to be 100 percent sure to move. If you're 80 percent clear, act. The rest will reveal itself through doing.

Use AI to support better decisions

AI won't replace your judgment, but it can sharpen it. Use it to:

- Generate options
- Compare scenarios
- Distill complexity

- Preview unintended consequences
- Clarify tradeoffs

Think of AI as a fast-thinking collaborator. You still make the call, but you don't have to think alone.

In a Grow in Beta world, progress matters more than precision. So stop waiting for the perfect. Start building your decision muscle one step, one signal, one move at a time.

Because beta decisions build real momentum.

Your "Decisions in Beta" Challenges

This week, use the micro-clarity framework to practice making decisions. Try one or more of the following:

The One-Sentence Goal

Write down one decision you're stuck on. Now describe the desired outcome in a single sentence. For example, I want to give my direct report feedback in a way that improves their performance without damaging trust. Or I want to prioritize one growth opportunity this quarter that will have the biggest long-term impact on my career.

The Facts vs. Assumptions Trial

Create two columns. In the first, list what you *know for sure* about your decision—data, deadlines, constraints, or confirmed inputs. In the second, list what you're *assuming*—timing, people's preferences, how things might go, or what success looks like. Then choose one assumption and clarify it. That might mean asking a stakeholder directly, running a quick test, or gut-checking it with a colleague.

The Small Move Drill

Pick one small, meaningful step you can take in the next forty-eight hours. It doesn't have to solve everything, just move you forward. Send an email to schedule a decision-making conversation. Sketch a rough outline of your plan. Ask one person for input.

The Lens Swap
Run your decision past a trusted peer, mentor, or AI tool. Ask a question that forces you to see it differently, like: "What's the risk I might be underestimating?" "If I were optimizing for speed, what would I do differently?"

24

Future-Proof Your Career

In a world shaped by rapid change, your career can't be a fixed road map. It needs to be a living prototype.

That's the mindset of Grow in Beta: You don't predict the future; you test your way into it.

A young client recently asked me, "How do I plan for a career when the job I'll have in ten years probably doesn't exist?"

It's a question I hear more and more, and not just from twentysomethings starting out. Mid-career professionals are asking it, too. Senior leaders are asking it. And almost all of them are asking it because of one force: artificial intelligence.

Trying to future-proof your career today feels a bit like packing for a trip when you don't know the destination, the weather, or how long you'll be gone. And there's a chance your travel companion is a robot who might replace you halfway through.

AI is changing the nature of work. Fast. Some jobs are disappearing. Others are being redesigned in real time. Entire fields—from marketing to medicine—are being reshaped by tools that can write, analyze, optimize, and predict with breathtaking speed.

A World Economic Forum report found that 39 percent of key skills required in the job market will change by 2030. Which means staying relevant won't come from locking into a single identity or title. It will come from your ability to evolve, to keep learning, and to reshape how your strengths show up in new contexts.

That kind of reinvention isn't about starting over. It's about staying in motion.

And that's where future-proofing comes in.

Don't Fear the Bots, Out-Human Them

Future-proofing your career isn't about competing with AI. It's about complementing it and knowing what only you can bring to the table.

Yes, AI can write reports, spot patterns, and process data at lightning speed. But it can't build trust. It can't resolve conflict. It can't hold space for uncertainty or help a team feel seen.

The most relevant professionals in the age of AI aren't the ones who automate the most. They're the ones who know when *not* to automate. They know which moments require more than output. They require presence.

That's why emotional intelligence, ethical reasoning, and relational adaptability are essential skills. They are the edge that sets you apart in a world where speed and scale are increasingly handled by machines.

Marcus had been in HR for over a decade. When his company rolled out AI tools to screen résumés, schedule interviews, and analyze engagement data, he welcomed the efficiency. At least at first. But soon, he began to wonder: *If the tools can do all this . . . what's left for me?*

He dove into the dashboards, trying to stay ahead of the curve. But the turning point came when tension flared between two senior managers. AI couldn't explain the conflict, let alone help resolve it.

Marcus could.

He used the AI insights to spot early signs of disengagement and pinpoint where communication had started to break down. But the real work happened in the room.

He brought the two leaders together and guided them through a tough, honest conversation. No scripts. No shortcuts. Just presence, empathy, and skilled facilitation. It wasn't fast or tidy, but it worked.

Afterward, one of them said, "I forgot how much people just want to feel understood."

So had Marcus.

That moment reminded him what can't be automated: trust, emotional intelligence, and the courage to navigate conflict. AI could support Marcus in navigating the issue. But it was Marcus's humanity that solved it.

Rethink What Security Really Means

Career security used to mean locking into one role and climbing the ladder. Today, that's a recipe for obsolescence.

In an AI-driven economy, security comes from adaptability: your ability to pivot, learn, and reinvent in response to change. That means letting go of rigid five-year plans in favor of five-day experiments. It means asking, "What's the smallest shift I can make this week to grow in a new direction?"

A friend of mine, who we'll call Dan, had worked at the same company for seventeen years. He'd moved steadily up the ladder—manager, director, senior director—and always thought of his title as a kind of armor. As long as he stayed loyal and kept delivering, he believed, his role would be safe. Then came the reorg. And the AI investments. Suddenly, entire workflows were being automated, and roles that once felt untouchable were quietly being phased out, including his.

To his credit, Dan didn't freeze. He started setting weekly goals: learning a new tool, reaching out to a contact, experimenting with how he framed his skill set. Within three months, he'd landed a new opportunity in a different industry, not because of his title but because of his mindset.

What saved him wasn't his résumé. It was his willingness to rethink what security really meant.

Reinvention Isn't a Reset

When people talk about reinventing themselves, they often imagine something dramatic: quitting everything, walking away from it all, starting from scratch. But in my experience, reinvention rarely looks like that. More often, it means building something new using what you already have.

I've reinvented my own career many times. Back in Chapter 2, I shared the highlights of my winding path, from musician to creative director to executive coach. But one reinvention stands out.

I began as a graphic designer. I loved the creativity, the problem-solving, the challenge of communicating visually. The truth is, I wasn't especially good at it.

What I discovered, though, was a growing interest in human behavior—how people think, connect, and adapt. That curiosity led me to pursue a master's degree in organizational behavior. But I didn't throw everything out and start over. I took a job in employee communications, where I could still use my creativity, just in a new way. I was designing conversations, not just visuals. I was shaping how people experienced their work environment.

That's what reinvention really is. Not a total reset, but a remix. In the new world of work, reinvention won't be a one-time pivot. It will be a career rhythm. You won't need to discard everything that came before. You'll need to find new ways to carry it forward.

Beta-Test Your Career

Let's get practical. If you want to thrive in the AI era, here are six ways to stay adaptable:

1. Build AI-aware skills

You don't need to become a prompt engineer or data scientist. But you *do* need to understand how AI is showing up in your field. Learn how it's used. Play with tools like Claude, a conversational AI similar to ChatGPT, or Midjourney, which generates images from text prompts. Ask yourself: *How can I use this to amplify my creativity, not replace it?*

2. Strengthen your human differentiators

AI can summarize data, but it can't inspire teams. It can optimize an email, but it can't build trust. Build on what truly sets you apart: empathy, storytelling, cross-functional collaboration, strategic judgment. These are your edge.

3. Treat curiosity as a career muscle

People who fear AI often stop learning. People who thrive with AI stay curious. Explore what's emerging. Don't wait to be trained; train yourself. Read about new tools. Join a webinar. Ask your team how they're using tech to work smarter.

4. Map transferable value

Don't define your career by a job title. Define it by what you *do well that creates value*. Can you build trust in tense situations? Help people feel seen and heard? Navigate ambiguity with empathy? Ask the uncomfortable questions others avoid? Create space where honesty and growth can happen? Those strengths can travel. AI may shift how they show up but not whether they matter.

5. Prototype your path

Don't wait for perfect clarity. Create multiple low-risk versions of your future: a tech-forward trajectory, a human-centered reinvention, a hybrid role you sketch out and test through side projects. Each version is a beta, and each one gives you feedback.

6. Collaborate with AI—don't compete against it

Use AI to co-create, co-edit, co-diagnose. Treat it like an intern with infinite knowledge but zero context or empathy. Train it to help you. The better you get at giving it direction, the more it becomes a tool, not a threat.

You don't need to outsmart the future. You just need to *stay in relationship* with it.

The most successful professionals I know are the ones who learn in public, prototype their path, and stretch their definition of success.

The future will reward those willing to try, tweak, and grow, one experiment at a time.

Your "Future-Proof Your Career" Challenges

Try one or more of these this week:

The AI Curiosity Search
Set a timer for fifteen minutes. Explore three AI tools relevant to your field. What might these tools *amplify*, not just automate?

The Five-Day Experiment
Pick one area of your work where you feel stuck or bored. Try one new approach, tool, or mindset for five days. What shifts?

The Reinvention Interview
Reach out to someone who's reinvented their career in the last five years. Ask them:

- What skills have proven most valuable in your new path?
- How did you navigate uncertainty or fear during the transition?
- If you had to reinvent yourself again today, what would you do differently?

Conclusion

You get to choose.

That's the truth most people forget when they talk about change, especially when they talk about AI. We treat it like a force of nature. Something inevitable. Unstoppable. Out of our hands.

But as technologist Tristan Harris points out, the way we deploy the world's most powerful technology isn't a given. It's a choice. And in a world where power is accelerating faster than our capacity to wield it wisely, the narrow path forward is the one where we match capability with responsibility, speed with reflection, and innovation with intention.

That's what this book has been about from the beginning.

Adaptability is not something outside of you. It's not just a response to change. It's a system: one you can understand, build, and strengthen. And it's a system that starts with you.

The Adaptability System: A Living Framework

As we've explored throughout this book, real adaptability requires both roots and branches:

- **Root to the Right Things**—Your roots. Your values, purpose, and strengths that keep you grounded when the winds of change blow hardest.

- **Prune the Loops**—The first branch. The hidden resistance patterns that quietly keep you stuck and how to break them.
- **Cultivate the Core Five**—The second branch. The five essential adaptability skills: curiosity, vulnerability, agility, flexibility, and resilience.
- **Grow in Beta**—The third branch. The daily habits, decisions, and experiments that keep your system evolving.

But what does it actually look like to live this system? Let's put the Adaptability System in motion through a few stories inspired by the real world that show how professionals apply these ideas in their work and life.

Sofia: Regrounding in a Storm

Sofia is a mid-level manager at a fast-scaling startup. The company is growing quickly, and so are the expectations. Overnight, she's asked to lead a new team, master a new project management tool, and integrate AI into her reporting process.

At first, she feels like she's drowning.

Then she remembers the tree.

She carves out an hour to reconnect to her roots. She rereads her personal values and purpose and realizes that her deepest motivation is creating clarity for others. That small moment grounds her.

Next, she maps her stressors and identifies a resistance loop: She keeps overplanning because she's afraid of looking unprepared. She interrupts that loop by testing a short kickoff meeting and gets positive feedback from her team. It wasn't perfect. But it was movement.

Drew: Stretching into the Unknown

Drew is a senior creative director at an agency where AI tools are being rolled out aggressively. Drew is skeptical and a little scared. Will AI replace the conceptual work they built their reputation on?

Instead of resisting, they get curious.

They set a challenge for themselves: experiment with one AI tool each week for a month to expand their thinking. In doing so, they start to see opportunities to delegate repetitive ideation tasks to the tool, freeing up time for deeper collaboration with their team.

They build agility by responding to a last-minute client ask with a co-created visual prototype in hours instead of days. And they flex emotionally when a younger colleague introduces a new tool they've never used, asking that colleague to teach them instead of pretending to already know.

They start leading a monthly "beta lunch," where the team shares what they're experimenting with. The vibe shifts from fear to fluency.

Malik: Rooted Reinvention

Malik is a senior insights analyst at a global consumer packaged goods company. He's known for his deep consumer knowledge, clean storytelling, and ability to spot market trends before they peak. But lately, the company has been shifting: reorganizations, pressure to adopt AI-driven analytics, and new leadership pushing for "leaner, faster, smarter" ways of working.

At first, Malik feels blindsided. His old methods—the ones that once made him a star—suddenly feel too slow, too manual, too "legacy."

But instead of defensiveness, Malik decides to apply the Adaptability System.

He revisits his roots. For Malik, it's not about holding on to the way things have always been. It's about advocating for insights that drive meaningful decisions. That's his why.

Then he takes a close look at his habits and sees that he's trapped in the Comfortably Stuck loop. He's been relying on familiar reporting structures even when they no longer serve the business.

So he prunes that loop away.

Instead of resisting the new AI platform, he gets curious. He asks for a peer tutorial, then builds his first prototype dashboard using AI to summarize voice-of-customer data. It's not perfect. But it's a start.

He stretches by practicing vulnerability: He shares the prototype with his manager and says, "This is new territory for me, but I want to lead here, not lag."

Malik also begins applying Grow in Beta thinking. He creates a standing thirty-minute "insight sprint" every Friday. It's a quick, no-polish session to surface patterns, reflect on what's working, and spot opportunities for improvement with one or two collaborators.

His influence grows, not because he changed who he is, but because he adapted how he works.

These stories aren't about perfection. They're about practice. About rooting deeper, stretching further, and growing a little more adaptable each day.

Like any healthy tree, your adaptability grows from the inside out. The soil it grows in? That's your context: your workplace, your team, your tools, your environment. But the system? That's you.

Which brings us to the final, and maybe most important, insight:

You Are the System

This isn't just a call to action. It's a recognition of power.

We often look to our company, our manager, or our industry to dictate how we should respond to change. But the truth is, you don't have to wait for permission to adapt. You don't need a new title, a new tool, or a new quarter to begin. The system you've been waiting for already exists.

It's you.

Your adaptability doesn't come from a program or a playbook. It comes from the choices you make every day:

- To pause when your instincts say panic
- To ask a question instead of offering an answer
- To say "I'm still learning" when perfectionism tries to shut you down
- To shift your system, not just your strategy

You are the roots. You are the branches. You are the one who decides what gets upgraded, what gets pruned, and what gets protected.

Human by Design

In a world increasingly shaped by algorithms, automation, and artificial intelligence, it's easy to forget what can't be digitized.

But adaptability isn't just about mastering AI prompts or learning the latest tools. It's about staying unmistakably human.

It's about what I remembered one recent weekend on a quiet trail in the Colorado mountains. No phone service. No calendar reminders. Just my breath, my boots, and the crunch of gravel underfoot. There was something about that hike— the way the trail curved unexpectedly, the way my legs ached on the climb but found rhythm in the descent—that reminded me: This is what it feels like to be alive. Present. Human.

That's the kind of adaptability we need. The kind that doesn't just respond to digital change but roots us in analog truths.

So build systems in your life that include the things technology can't replicate: hikes, handwritten notes, slow dinners, coffee with friends, conversations without an agenda. Eye contact. Art. Silence.

Because the most advanced system you'll ever design won't be a platform or productivity hack.

It's your own humanity.

That's what will set you apart. That's what will keep you grounded. That's what will keep you growing.

And maybe, just like that unexpected switchback on the trail, it's what will lead you somewhere entirely new.

From Me to You

If you've made it this far in the book, thank you.

Thank you for being willing to stretch. For thinking critically about how you respond to change. For seeing adaptability not just as a work skill but as a way of living with more agency, more compassion, and more intention.

I wrote this book not because I have all the answers, but because I needed to ask the questions. At different points in my life and career, I've clung too tightly to my expertise. I've confused productivity with progress. I've held on to routines and roles that no longer reflected my values. I've clung to certainty at the expense of facts. I've resisted change not because I didn't understand it, but because I feared what it might ask of me. And I've broken, rebuilt, questioned, and relearned more times than I can count.

But every time I came back to this truth: You don't have to be perfect to adapt. You just have to stay in motion. With intention. With heart. With the courage to keep evolving, even when the outcome is uncertain.

That's the system.

And you're already running it, imperfectly, beautifully, your way.

So begin again.

Root to what matters.

Stretch toward what's next.

And bend, don't break.

Notes

Chapter 1: The End of Expertise

Need for adaptability, conflict navigation, innovative thinking skills rising: LinkedIn (2023). "2023 Workplace Learning Report." https://learning.linkedin.com/resources/workplace-learning-report-2023

Adaptability is one of the most in-demand traits globally: Microsoft & LinkedIn (2025). "2025 Work Trend Index Annual Report 2025: The year the Frontier Firm is born." https://www.microsoft.com/en-us/worklab/work-trend-index/2025-the-year-the-frontier-firm-is-born

Chapter 2: The Adaptability Paradox

Megginson summarizes Darwin's thinking that adaptability determines survival: L. C. Megginson (1963). "Lessons from Europe for American Business." *Southwestern Social Science Quarterly,* 44(1): 3–13.

Chapter 3: Identity Protection

Employee fears about AI replacing not just skills but identity and value in the workplace: World Economic Forum (2023). "The Future of Jobs Report 2023." https://www.weforum.org/reports/the-future-of-jobs-report-2023/

Chapter 4: How to Not Break

*Digital overload and constant change are driving burnout and
    exhaustion at work:* Microsoft (2025). "Microsoft 2025 annual
    Work Trend Index." https://news.microsoft.com/annual-work
    -trend-index-2025/

Chapter 8: Choose Your Roots

Book that challenges to clarify what matters most: Stephen R.
    Covey, *The 7 Habits of Highly Effective People: Powerful Lessons
    in Personal Change* (Free Press, 1989).

Chapter 9: Build Your Inner Capacity

"To tame it, name it" approach: Brené Brown, *Atlas of the Heart:
    Mapping Meaningful Connection and the Language of Human
    Experience* (Random House, 2021).

Chapter 16: Credible Vulnerability

Vulnerability is a foundation of courage: Brené Brown, *Dare
    to Lead: Brave Work. Tough Conversations. Whole Hearts*
    (Random House, 2018).
Leaders who expressed vulnerability seen as more trustworthy:
    R. C. Mayer & M. B. Gavin (2005). "Trust in Management
    and Performance: Who Minds the Shop While the Employees
    Watch the Boss?" *Academy of Management Journal*, 48(5):
    874–888.

Chapter 18: Emotional and Cognitive Flexibility

Emotional suppression as a cause of professional burnout:
    M. Rodriguez & J. Park (2024). "Emotional Suppression and

Professional Burnout: A Longitudinal Study." *Journal of Occupational Health Psychology*, 29(2): 156–171.

Emotional regulation skills in high-stakes performance environments: R. Williams & K. Chen (2024). "Emotional Regulation in High-Stakes Medical Settings." *Journal of Applied Psychology*, 109(2): 234–249.

Emotional elasticity in organizational leadership: L. Thompson & K. Martinez (2023). "Emotional Elasticity in Organizational Leadership: A Study of 500 Executives." *Management Science Quarterly*, 45(3): 312–328.

Flexibility among the most important workplace skills of the future: World Economic Forum. "The Future of Jobs Report 2023." https://www.weforum.org/publications/the-future-of-jobs-report-2023

Cognitive flexibility is a foundation of adaptable thinking: D. R. Dajani & L. Q. Uddin (2015). "Demystifying cognitive flexibility: Implications for clinical and developmental neuroscience." *Trends in Neurosciences*, 38(9): 571–578.

Growth mindset is a psychological basis for adaptability: Carol S. Dweck, *Mindset: The New Psychology of Success* (Random House, 2006).

Chapter 19: Resilience That Moves Forward

Stress that doesn't get addressed doesn't go away; it just gets heavier: University of Minnesota (n.d.). "Building Work Stress Resilience." University of Minnesota Human Resources. https://hr.umn.edu/supervising/resources/Building-Work-Stress-Resilience

Resilient employees report higher job satisfaction: M. K. Shoss, L. Jiang & T. M. Probst (2016). "Bending without breaking: A two-study examination of employee resilience in the face of job insecurity." *Journal of Occupational Health Psychology*, 21(4): 453–469. https://doi.org/10.1037/ocp0000060

Chapter 20: Upgradeable by Design

Half of employers name AI the top force reshaping job roles and skills: World Economic Forum (2025). "The Future of Jobs Report 2025." https://www.weforum.org/reports/the-future-of-jobs-report-2025/

Systems thinking is "a discipline for seeing wholes": Peter M. Senge, *The Fifth Discipline: The Art & Practice of the Learning Organization*, rev. ed. (Doubleday/Currency, 2006).

You don't rise to the level of your goals; you fall to the level of your systems: James Clear, *Atomic Habits: An Easy & Proven Way to Build Good Habits & Break Bad Ones* (Avery, 2018).

Chapter 21: Feedback Is Signal, Not Judgment

People who actively seek feedback tend to be higher performers: S. J. Ashford & A. S. Tsui (1991). "Self-regulation for managerial effectiveness: The role of active feedback seeking." *Academy of Management Journal*, 34(2): 251–280.

Chapter 22: Break Up with Perfect

AI agents tend to affirm whatever we say, rather than offering friction: E. Mollick (2024). "Personality and Persuasion." *One Useful Thing.* https://www.oneusefulthing.org/p/personality-and-persuasion

Chapter 23: Decisions in Beta

Professionals who master fast, adaptive decision-making are twice as likely to make high-quality decisions: McKinsey & Company (April 30, 2019). "Decision making in the age of urgency."

https://www.mckinsey.com/capabilities/people-and
-organizational-performance/our-insights/decision-making
-in-the-age-of-urgency

Chapter 24: Future-Proof Your Career

More than one-third of key skills required in the job market will
change by 2030: World Economic Forum (2025). "The Future of
Jobs Report 2025." https://www.weforum.org/publications/the
-future-of-jobs-report-2025/

Conclusion: You Are the System

The way we use AI isn't a given—it's a choice: T. Harris (April 2025).
"Why AI Is Our Ultimate Test and Greatest Invitation." TED
Talk, Vancouver, BC. https://www.youtube.com/watch?v
=6kPHnl-RsVI

Acknowledgments

No one bends alone. This book only exists because of the support, generosity, and brilliance of the people who shaped both me and the work.

First, to the team at **Girl Friday**: Kristin Duran, Karen Upson, Georgie Hockett, Kylee Hayes, and so many others, thank you for your editorial wisdom, marketing brilliance, and behind-the-scenes magic. I couldn't have asked for a better group to help bring this book into the world. You made everything stronger, cleaner, and more human.

To **Kelly Madrone**, thank you for your steady hand, sharp insight, and ability to help me turn rough ideas into something real. You were the developmental backbone of this book, and I'm grateful for your early guidance.

Jeevan Sivasubramaniam, your unexpected and generous feedback came at exactly the right time. Your encouragement to center around a core philosophy helped me write more clearly and honestly.

Dave Duschene and **Linda Kingman**, thank you for being extraordinary leaders, mentors, examples, and friends. Your influence shaped not only this book but my entire career. I hope you both know how much that means. Now . . . when's our next breakfast?

Gary Rudnick, under your tough exterior is one of the most compassionate hearts in this business. Thank you for trusting me, for giving me space and support, and for believing in my work.

To **Jeff Beringer, Joe Leslie, Alexandra Ladas**, and **David Lance**, thank you for sharing your valuable perspectives on AI and supporting my thinking.

Deborah Grayson Riegel, thank you for your publishing and speaking wisdom and your generous mentorship.

Charlie Hughes-Jones, Alyssa Fu Ward, Kimaada Brown, and **Rebecca Rieschl**, thank you for being brilliant, grounded, and generous humans. I'm lucky to be a part of our little band of optimists.

Mark Strong and **Jurene Fremstad**, thank you for your early encouragement to write this book. Your enthusiasm helped me take the leap.

Daniel Pitlik, thank you for your mentorship, friendship, and endless support. Whether you know it or not, you are the chair of my Board of Directors. You help me feel a little less lost on this wild ride. Let's hang out on your next Daniel Day.

To **Clifton O'Neal**, thank you for taking a chance on someone with a red pen and a smidgen of potential. That moment changed everything for me.

To **Noel Paterson** (my big bro) and **Delia Berrigan Fakis**, thank you for your generous legal wisdom. You helped me move forward with confidence.

To the many incredible people I've had the privilege of coaching and training over the years, thank you for your vulnerability, your stories, and your willingness to stretch. You continue to show me what adaptability looks like in real life, and I am endlessly inspired by you.

To my **mom**. You were messy, hilarious, and full of contradictions. The older I get, the more I understand. I hope you finally found that suitcase of money in the sky.

And to **Karen**, my person in life and love. You've stood beside me through every bend, reset, and overthink. Thank you for your humor, your selflessness, and your ride-or-die presence, even when I'm tired, hangry, or spiraling. I find you infinitely fascinating, and even more so with each chapter we write together.

About the Author

Photo © Aaron Pagaza

Matt A. West is a leadership coach, facilitator, trainer, speaker, and consultant who has spent over two decades helping people and organizations grow stronger in times of change. Drawing on a mix of learning and development, communications strategy, organizational behavior, and creative design, his work has taken him inside some of the world's most recognizable organizations, including Walmart, Facebook, Adobe, McDonald's, Unilever, Johnson & Johnson, Kraft Foods, PepsiCo, Cisco, and Kaiser Permanente.

He is executive vice president of coaching and facilitation at Golin, a leading global public relations agency. Matt holds a master of science in management and organizational behavior and a bachelor of arts in communications. He is also credentialed by the Association for Talent Development (ATD) as a Certified Professional in Learning and Performance and by the International Coaching Federation (ICF) as a coach, and he is an award-winning member of Toastmasters International. In addition, he is a frequent lecturer at the University of Colorado Boulder and Loyola University Chicago.

Bend, Don't Break is his first book.

www.ingramcontent.com/pod-product-compliance
Lightning Source LLC
Chambersburg PA
CBHW022050020426

42335CB00012B/626